THE BLACK WRITER
IN
AFRICA AND THE AMERICAS

Edited
and with an introduction
by

LLOYD W. BROWN

HENNESSEY & INGALLS, INC.
Los Angeles   1973

CONTENTS

INTRODUCTION

The papers in this volume were originally delivered at the University of Southern California's Fourth Annual Conference on Comparative Literature in April 1970. In recent years the usual symposium on Black Literature has been one of our more popular academic spectacles—*respectable* exhibition, admittedly, but an exhibition nonetheless. Of course, there has always been something of the exhibitionistic in the very nature of any conference. As organizers we are not simply preoccupied with providing a forum for informative discussion, useful ideas, and constructive programs, we also seek, naturally enough, to offer everything in an attractive

1

Lloyd W. Brown

package as an entertaining spectacle. And, in our anxious postmortems, the "success" of the conference is measured implicitly or otherwise by its worth as a spectator sport as well as by its intellectual contributions, if any. In Academe the conference on Black literature is a rather special example of this kind of showmanship. After all, the subject is a natural: in the context of the academic establishment, Black literature is still a strange, though far from new creature— something which has always been undeniably present, but which is only now being perceived, however darkly. Hence, whenever the "experts" gather, especially if they are Black artists and Black scholars, the usual spectacle takes on the dimensions of a very special exhibit to be inspected, sympathetically and otherwise, by the academic community. As for the experts themselves, *their* spectator value is derived not only from the traditional enlightenment-cum-entertainment of all conferences, but also from the political spectrum of the race problem, the titillating rivalries of militants-versus-moderates-versus-Uncle Toms, and so on.

However, we witnessed something of a reversal of this spectator principle in the Black literature conference sponsored by the Graduate School and Comparative Literature Program at the University of Southern California: although Black literature was on display as usual, it soon became clear that the focal point of the spectacle was the academic community itself. As the papers here demonstrate, participants were addressing themselves not simply to Black literature as such, but to the literary principles and particularly the aesthetic criteria which have been dominant in the

2

(White) literary establishment. In effect, much of the conference concerned itself with the establishment's usual reaction, or more precisely, with its notorious lack of response, to Black literature. This traditional failure and its historical causes are axiomatic, and the conference participants were not, consciously at any rate, about to belabor the obvious or to recite truisms for their own sake. What they were seeking were viable alternatives to an acknowledged history of neglect and blindness. In the process, these scholars, Black and White, were passing deliberate judgment on the academic profession vis-à-vis the Black experience. They were also, however inadvertently, the principal actors in an always intriguing drama. The variety of solutions, propositions, and viewpoints which they offered reenacted the universities' belated and still underdeveloped responses to Black literature. Hence, the divergent points of view which some of these papers represent reflect the deep-seated conflicts within the academic community itself; these were the conflicts that formed the spectacle of our Black literature conference.

The crucial issue in controversies of this kind is not only Black literature itself, but the Black aesthetic, and it has become increasingly clear that any attempt to study the former must begin with the challenge of the latter—a challenge that questions the relevancy of traditional (White) aesthetics to the Black writer. Black critics and artists such as Hoyt Fuller, editor of the *Black World* journal, and Larry Neal, coeditor (with LeRoi Jones) of the *Black Fire* anthology, have bluntly declared the irrelevancy of critical standards that are rooted in traditions of White, Western intellectuality. According to these critics, Blacks and Whites belong to distinctively different cultures, each with its "own way of looking at the world." This challenge provoked the kinds of reaction which were discussed at the University of Southern California conference. It accounts for fearful vituperation about "racial chauvinism" just as much as it explains earnest attempts to demonstrate (a) the "respectability" of Black literature as a "serious" academic discipline and (b) the relevance of traditional methodology in the evaluation of Black literature.

However, in the final analysis both tactics are evasive. Mere invectives do not meet the gut issues that the Black aesthetic raises about the very nature of prevailing literary and cultural definitions. Like it or not, the Black aesthetic is a fact, one that cannot be wished or abused into oblivion. Similarly, those who merely emphasize the relevance of certain methodological principles to Black literature are also obfuscating the issues. They are really engaged in a kind of erudite side stepping, for the Black aesthetic is not questioning the usefulness of the mechanical apparatus of literary criticism (textual analysis, close reading, structural investigation, and so on). What is being questioned is the relevance of those value systems to which this investigative machinery has been applied in traditional literary criticism. The Black nationalist is calling for a frank recognition of ethnic (i.e., Black) perspectives in Black literature in preference to familiar (i.e., White) notions of "universality," and he is asking for functional definitions of literature to replace a traditionally esoteric emphasis ("art for art's sake," or "literature as literature"). All of this is not to deny the good intentions behind the methodological issue. Alas, it still seems necessary to persuade some quarters that Black literature, or much of it, is capable of sustaining rigorous textual analysis. But when so much important work remains neglected in the study of Black literature itself, the critic needs to establish meaningful priorities, and at this time, the intransigent backwoods of the academic community are highly questionable as the critic's number one priority. Moreover, in view of the fact that the Black aesthetic does not reject analytical methods per se, the issue of evaluative techniques is somewhat gratutious. The earnest arguments of the methodologist are just as irrelevant as the vituperative labels of the name callers.

These evasive tactics still form a significant part of the reaction to the Black aesthetic, a depressing revelation because they reflect, on the evidence published thus far, the dominant attitudes toward the subject in those circles of the academic community which pride themselves on their ability and willingness to become truly engaged in Black literature. The established forms of evasion or obfuscation have perpetuated the vacuum which has always existed in academic approaches to Black literature and which the current avowals of interest and understanding purport to destroy. This intellectual void also explains those glaring gaps in scholarship and research which are emphasized rather than closed by the current flood of publications. These "new" publications are almost always exploitive rather than contributive. In the absence of competent and innovative scholarship, it has been all but impossible to realize a creative forum of ideas about Black literature in the academic community. (However, as the emergence of the Black aesthetic itself suggests, there has been no such dearth in the community of Black artists.) Instead of a forum, we have a huckster's market place of repetitious anthologies, endless reprints and excerpts from the same, safe standards (e.g., Baldwin's *Notes of a Native Son* and Robert Bone's *Negro Novel*), and well worn standard approaches to a limited range of topics (violence in *Native Son*, universality or structure in *Invisible Man,* protest in Baldwin, and alleged monomania in LeRoi Jones's *The Slave*). The academic critic has limited himself to a continuous replay of familiar voices on tired themes. He cannot hear the "new" Black voices, or if he does, he does not understand them.

This explains why little or no work has been done on LeRoi Jones (apart from the usual dogmatic invectives) despite the fact that it is impossible to grasp the full implications of the "Black Revolution" in literature without studying Jones and his fellow writers of the sixties and seventies. This also explains why the scholarship on earlier periods is either shallow or nonexistent. The narrow obsession with a small coterie of writers in the forties and fifties has given rise to absurd notions about Black literature before *Native Son.* It is becoming increasingly fashionable, for example, to see the forties and after as a period of resurgence or renaissance in Black literature. We need to ask (and there was a similar need in the twenties apropos of the so-called

Harlem Renaissance) whether such labels are not gratuitous, whether it is not the academic community rather than the Black writer that is now experiencing a renaissance—and not a very impressive one at that. In fact, there is no dearth of exciting, significant, or complex Black writings before the twenties and the forties. What is lacking is the awareness that such works exist. Obviously, the academic renaissance is hardly underway, and as far as Black literature is concerned, it will not be complete until or unless the critic realizes the extent to which the Black aesthetic challenges not only the traditional academic approaches to Black writing as such, but also certain standards of literary criticism as a whole.

On what basis, for example, do we determine the significance of Black or of any literature before, during, or after the forties? Is it in relation to some expressive, symbolical value? Is significance determined by a narrowly qualitative standard, by an elitist dogma which defines good literature as classic or great writing, and which evaluates literary scholarship not only in terms of content, but also in terms of prestigious presses, noncommercial publishers, and respectable journals? Let us interject here, without equivocation, that Wright, Ellison, and Baldwin *are* enormously significant writers by all the connotations (qualitative, expressive, and so on) of that overworked word. However, the almost exclusive emphasis on *them*, even now during the academic renaissance, implies that the critic's awakening is little more than a somnolent reflex, an unthinking, automatic application of an elitist philosophy which has prospered for generations in the criticism of European and (White) American literatures. What about that hallowed old humbug, the universalist doctrine? Harold Cruse (*Rebellion or Revolution*), LeRoi Jones (*Home*), and a host of less significant (?) writers have confirmed what some of us have suspected in the past: the universal standards and ideals on which the academic critic places such a high premium are Western constructs. The revolt against *this* universalist dogma is not a rejection of universalism as such: Fanon (*Wretched of the Earth*), Jones (*Black Mass*), and, before them, DuBois (*Darkwater*) all call for a flexible definition of universality that encompasses and encourages tolerant forms of individual, national, and ethnic consciousness.

The real target of the present revolt is an ethnocentric definition of *universal* which, to quote Richard Gilman, flourishes "under the great flawless arc of the Graeco-Roman and Judaeo-Christian traditions" (*New Republic*, March 9, 1968). Inevitably, the relationship between Black literature and the academic establishment has become a microcosm of the wider relationship between Blacks and White society. In challenging the institutionalized racism of White society, the civil rights movement and the Black nationalists have raised questions about the *total* structure of the society. Now, the challenge of the Black aesthetic reaches beyond the relationship between Black literature and academic standards to question the very nature of academic assumptions about literature in general.

Nor can the field of comparative literature escape this kind of challenge. On the whole, satisfactory de jure definitions of comparative literature have been in very short supply, but there is no denying that there is an established, de facto definition—comparative literature as Western (i.e., White) literature—which is a natural offshoot of White, ethnocentric assumptions about literature and aesthetics. Yet, ironically, this is the very field in which Blacks and students of the Black experience should have a special interest, for the Black man's history of involuntary migration—the "Black Diaspora," if you will—has given him a very important stake in a genuinely comparative, rather than spuriously universal study of cultures.

The conference papers by Mercer Cook, Austin Clarke, and Ismith Khan demonstrate the cultural similarities which link Blacks from Africa, the Caribbean, and North America, and which originate with (a) the common factor of White racism and (b) the unifying memories, however faint, of an African heritage. Altogether, a comparative study of literature which frees itself from the old White parochialism can shed much light on the cultural links (a) within a non-White ethnic group and (b) between such a group and the pervasive White culture. As far as Black literature is concerned, the papers presented here give some inkling of a formidable variety of topics within a Pan-African framework: Negritude and Soul, language and identity, the calypso tradition in the Caribbean and Latin America, Pan-African mythology and folklore, the Blues in literature, and the Black rebel (the ethos of the Black Revolution). Then there are the accompanying issues and archetypes which shape the Afro-European tradition: the Prospero-Caliban myth (the psychopathology of racism and colonialism), Marxism, Existentialism,

Lloyd W. Brown

Judaeo-Christian mythology, the messianic tradition (especially the Black Christ archetype), and, indeed, the very issue of *tradition* itself (the relation of Black heritage and identity to White definitions of history and tradition). The possibilities are unlimited. They deserve something more creative than the self-serving limitations of past and present scholarship.

CONCEPTS OF THE BLACK AESTHETIC IN CONTEMPORARY BLACK LITERATURE

Abraham Chapman

The **Black aesthetic** has emerged as a new term in Black literary and political publications in the United States, stressing the existence and still undeveloped potentials of a unique and distinctive culture created by Black people. The Black arts, in the view of the proponents of the Black aesthetic, grow out of this culture which is rooted in the Black experience in the United States and throughout the world. The Black experience includes the historical roots and beginnings in Africa with its cultures and arts; the involuntary transatlantic crossing; the experience of slavery and the resistance to it; the systems of racism, oppression, and

11

segregation in the United States, which deprive Black people of the conditions for the free fulfillment of their personalities and lives; and the significant inner resources created and developed by Black Americans to affirm, express, and develop their humanity and individual personalities in a dehumanizing and depersonalizing environment.

The Black aesthetic expresses the original life-styles, rhythms, images, sensibilities, music, and languages of Black people in Africa and the West.

In one of his speeches, the Black West Indian novelist George Lamming defined Black as "synonymous with originating in Africa." The Black aesthetic, on its most literal level of meaning, is an aesthetic of African origin which evolved in its own ways in the course of interaction with other cultures and aesthetics as Black people inhabited larger stretches of the world outside of Africa.

W. E. B. DuBois' well-known work, *The Souls of Black Folk* (1903), describes the development of the slave songs in three stages of development:

> The first is African music, the second Afro-American, while the third is a blending of Negro music with the music heard in the foster land. The result is still distinctively Negro and the method of blending original, but the elements are both Negro and Caucasian. One might go further and find a fourth step in this development, where the songs of white America have been distinctively influenced by the slave songs . . .[1]

In effect, he is emphasizing the kind of syncretism which preserves the original styles and character of Black people.

Such cultural interaction must be distinguished from cultural genocide.

The Black aesthetic is still in the process of being defined and developed, frequently in association with kindred concepts like the "literature of combat" or "the culture of revolution," by vigorous and vocal groups of contemporary Black artists and critics. It appears not only as a critical term and cultural concept, but has been described by Hoyt W. Fuller, the critic and managing editor of *Negro Digest* (now *Black World*), as "the new movement toward 'a black aesthetic' and the preoccupation with 'the black experience,' aspects of the larger Black Consciousness Movement."[2]

As a movement it has been manifest in the birth and proliferation of Black cultural media directed and produced by and for Black people in all parts of Black America. The number of Black literary and political periodicals has grown so rapidly and extensively that it is practically impossible today even to keep track of all of them. Older publications like *Negro Digest, Freedomways,* and *Liberator* are in the movement. *The Journal of Black Poetry,* edited by Joe Goncalves in San Francisco since 1966, has become the first sustained and continuous magazine of Black poetry in the history of Afro-American literature. Black literary and political publications which can be considered part of the Black aesthetic movement are *Soulbook; Black Dialogue; Black Expression; Dasein; Free Lance; Uhuru; Umbra; Umbra Anthology; ex umbra; Nommo,* the journal of the OBAC (Organization of Black American Culture) Writer's Workshop in Chicago; *Nkombo,* the literary journal published quarterly by BLKARTSOUTH of the Free Southern Theatre in New Orleans; and *The Black Arts* quarterly. *Black Theatre,* published in Harlem by New Lafayette Theatre, is a recent periodical devoted to the publication of plays, drama, criticism, and news of the Black theatre movement. *The Cricket* is a recent publication devoted to Black music, edited by the Black writers LeRoi Jones, Larry Neal, and A. B. Spellman. In California, Nathan Hare has established and publishes *The Black Scholar,* a new journal of Black studies and scholarly research.

Black publishing houses, concentrating largely on Black poetry, have emerged in many parts of the country. The oldest and best known is Broadside Press in Detroit, founded in 1965 by its editor-director, poet Dudley Randall. In Newark, Jihad Productions publishes political and literary material and issues records of new Black music. In New Orleans, BLKARTSOUTH of the Free Southern Theatre publishes volumes of verse in addition to the journal *Nkombo.* In Chicago, Third World Press and Free Black Press have appeared. In San Francisco, Black literature is being published by Julian Richardson Associates and the Journal of Black Poetry Press. In Washington, D.C., Drum and Spear Press has been launched.

Black theater groups, too numerous to be counted, have been organized and are performing throughout the United States. Black bookshops have been established in Black communities where they never existed before. Black arts festivals are now quite common in colleges and Black communities.

All these new Black cultural media are dedicated to the beauty of Blackness and are distinguished by their determination to be free of White editors and White direction and to be controlled by Blacks. Black aesthetic is not an abstract term. It is a term reflecting the dynamics of cultural change in the Black communities today, and it is winning increasing recognition among Black intellectuals. The March 1970 issue of *Negro Digest* published the "Statement of Purpose of the Institute of the Black World," the second element of the Martin Luther King Jr. Memorial Center to be created in Atlanta. Its central thrust, as the statement explains, is "the creation of an international center for Black Studies, with strong emphasis on research, broadly conceived." The statement lists ten basic program elements, the second of which is the following:

> The encouragement of those creative artists who are searching for the meaning of a black aesthetic, who are now trying to define and build the basic ground out of which black creativity may flow in the arts. Encounter among these artists on the one hand, and scholars, activists, and students on the other, must be constant, in both formal and informal settings.

What we have been witnessing so far is only the beginning of the Black aesthetic movement in the United States, a movement which is clearly in ferment and in the process of development as well as in the throes of impassioned debate between Black opponents and proponents and diverse views among its proponents.

15

Like all aesthetic terms which have become the banners of literary and cultural movements, it is not a purely aesthetic concept and it does not mean the same thing to everybody who uses it. It is closely linked with the ideological and political currents of thought manifest in the new forms of consciousness and struggle of the Black liberation movement in the U.S., particularly Black nationalism and cultural nationalism. Contemporary Black nationalism has undoubtedly influenced the growth of the Black aesthetic. However, the Black American's aesthetic concepts can be traced to an older and international movement which, in turn, originated with the history of Afro-European relationships. This is the history of Africans and their descendants in the Western world rejecting Western colonialism and racism, assumptions which Frantz Fanon described as "the doctrine of cultural hierarchy."[3] Fanon saw the "doctrine of cultural hierarchy" as an important element of the colonialism and racism which have traditionally negated, derogated, "inferiorized," and sought to destroy the cultures of all colonized groups.

A short passage from David Hume's *Philosophical Works* (1748) illustrates how deeply ingrained White ethnocentricism has been in the allegedly rational traditions of Western philosophy:

> I am apt to suspect the negroes, and in general all the other species of men (for there are four or five different kinds) to be naturally inferior to the whites. There never was a civilized nation of any

other complexion than white, nor even any individual eminent either in action or speculation. No ingenious manufactures amongst them, no arts, no sciences. On the other hand, the most rude and barbarous of the whites, such as the ancient Germans, the present Tartars, have still something eminent about them, in their valour, form of government, or some other particular. Such a uniform and constant difference could not happen in so many countries and ages, if nature had not made an original distinction betwext these breeds of men . . . . In Jamaica indeed they talk of one negroe as a man of parts and learning; but 'tis likely he is admired for very slender accomplishments, like a parrot, who speaks a few words plainly.[4]

Blacks throughout the world have been opposing such views ever since their first experience of White racism. An early example of this protest is a missionary pamphlet published in Philadelphia in 1800: *The Black Prince.* This is the biography account of an African prince who was brought to England in 1791 for a Christian education, and it demonstrates how his African values were to be destroyed before he could be converted to Christianity:

He [Naimbana] was present once in the House of Commons during a debate on the slave trade. He there heard a gentleman, who spoke in favour of the trade, say some things very degrading to the character of his countrymen. He was so enraged at this, that on coming out of the House, he cried out with great vehemence, "I will kill that fellow

17

wherever I meet him, for he has told lies of my country." He was put in mind of the Christian duty of forgiving his enemies, on which he answered nearly in the the following words: "If a man should rob me of my money, I can forgive him; if a man should shoot at me, I can forgive him; if a man should sell me and all my family to a slave ship, so that we should pass all the rest of our lives in slavery in the West Indies, I can forgive him; but," added he with much emotion, "if a man takes away the character of the people of my country, I never can forgive him." Being asked why he would not extend his forgiveness to one who took away the character of the people of his country, he answered, "If a man should try to kill me, or should sell my family for slaves, he would do an injury to as many as he might kill or sell, but if any one takes away the character of black people, that man injures black people all over the world; and when he has once taken away their character, there is nothing which he may not do to black people ever after. That man, for instance, will beat black men, and say, 'O, it is only a black man, why should I not beat him!' That man will make slaves of black people; for when he has taken away their character he will say, 'O, they are only black people, why should not I make them slaves.' That man will take away all the people of Africa, if he can catch them, and if you ask him, 'but why do you take away all these people,' he will say, 'O, they are only black people, they are not like white people, why should not I take them?' That is the reason why I cannot forgive the man who takes away the character of the people of my country." [5]

The contemporary concepts of the Black aesthetic continue this traditional defense against White attempts to rob Blacks of their culture. So does the Black nationalist element in the contemporary Black liberation movement.

One of the chief champions and architects of the Black aesthetic movement is LeRoi Jones who has changed his name to Ameer Baraka. He has expressed his views on the Black aesthetic in articles, lectures, interviews, and poems and has embodied the Black aesthetic, as he perceives it, in plays, poems, and fiction. In one of the last essays in his book, *Home,* he wrote:

> The song title "A White Man's Heaven Is a Black Man's Hell" describes how complete an image reversal is necessary in the West. Because for many Black people, the white man has succeeded in making this hell seem like heaven. But Black youth are much better off in this regard than their parents. They are the ones who need the least image reversal.

> The Black artist, in this context, is desperately needed to change the images his people identify with, by asserting Black feeling, Black mind, Black judgment. The Black intellectual, in this same context, is needed to change the interpretation of facts toward the Black Man's best interests, instead of merely tagging along reciting white judgments of the world.[6]

Hoyt W. Fuller, in a 1968 article in the magazine, *The Critic,* voiced the following view:

> Central to the problem of the irreconcilable conflict between the black writer and the white critic

is the failure of recognition of a fundamental and
obvious truth of American life—that the two races
are residents of two separate and naturally antagonistic worlds. No manner of well-meaning rhetoric
about "one country" and "one people" and even
about the two races' long joint-occupancy of this
troubled land, can obliterate the high, thick
dividing walls which hate and history have
erected—and maintain—between them . . . . Black
Americans are for all practical purposes, colonized
in their native land . . . . After centuries of being
told, in a million different ways, that they were
not beautiful, and that whiteness of skin, straight-
ness of hair, and aquilinity of features constituted
the only measures of beauty, black people have
revolted . . . . In Chicago, the Organization of
Black American Culture has moved boldly toward
a definition of a black aesthetic. In the writer's
workshop sponsored by the group, the writers are
deliberately striving to invest their work with the
distinctive styles and rhythms and colors of the
ghetto, with those peculiar qualities which, for
example, characterize the music of a John
Coltrane, or a Charlie Parker or a Ray Charles.[7]

In an article in the first issue of *Nommo,* the OBAC
literary journal launched in the winter of 1969, Hoyt Fuller,
who is the advisor of the organization, wrote:

Generations of black Americans have lived out
their lives seeing themselves through the eyes of
white men. Even today, millions of black Americans evaluate their worthiness according to their
approximation—in skin color, in morals, in outlook,

in ambitions—of white standards. What they say to themselves, in effect, is this: I approach wholeness as a human being to the degree that I look and think and behave like white people . . . .

What the writers of the OBAC Writers' Workshop are attempting, simply, is to write naturally and honestly out of their own experiences, rejecting the counsel of the critics and the university professors that they concern themselves with "universals." And, in doing this, they are— wittingly or unwittingly, it does not matter— moving toward a black aesthetic.[8]

In the opening essay in the anthology *Black Fire,* James T. Stewart, a Philadelphia writer, artist, and musician, discussed "the development of the black revolutionary artist" today and stated:

The dilemma of the "negro" artist is that he makes assumptions based on the wrong models. He makes assumptions based on white models. These assumptions are not only wrong, they are even antithetical to his existence. The black artist must construct models which correspond to his own reality. The models must be non-white. Our models must be consistent with a black style, our natural aesthetic styles, and our moral and spiritual styles. In doing so, we will be merely following the natural demands of our culture. These demands are suppressed in the larger (white) culture, but, nonetheless, are found in our music and in our spiritual and moral philosophy. Particularly in music, which happens to be the purest expression of the black

man in America . . . . We are, in essence, the
ingredients that will create the future. For this
reason, we are misfits, estranged from the white
cultural present. This is our position as black artists
in these times. Historically and sociologically we
are the rejected. Therefore, we must know that we
are the building stones for the New Era.[9]

In a special article written for the anthology *Black
Expression* on the Black poetry movement today, Dudley
Randall observed:

When two of the Broadside poets were asked for
poems for a new little magazine, they refused,
saying they preferred not to appear in a white
publication.. . . The younger poets no longer plead,
or ask for rights from the white man. Instead of
searching themselves for faults which engender the
contempt of the white man, and, after regarding
his wars, his hypocritical religion, his exploitation,
his dehumanization, they dub him—"the Beast."
They no longer pity themselves . . . . Instead, they
say, "I am black and beautiful." They reject
whiteness and white standards. They call themselves blacks, rejecting the word Negro, which they
say was given to them by white men. Some poets
have taken African names. Le Graham is now
Ahmed Alhamisi, Roland Snellings is Asaka
Muhammad Touré.

This intensified pride in blackness has made the
new poets indifferent to a white audience. [He lists
a series of black publications as] periodicals where
they can publish for a black audience without
white censorship . . . . Writing for a black audience

out of black experience, the poets seek to make their work relevant and to direct their audience to black consciousness, black unity, and black power. This may be called didacticism or propaganda, but they are indifferent to labels put upon it. They consider such labels as part of white standards, and they reject white standards . . . . In spite of my emphasis on the black consciousness of the poets, I do not wish to leave the impression of a monolithic sameness. There are all shades of opinion and militancy among the poets. Some are proudly black, and others would prefer to be colorless. In fact, just as the two Broadside poets refused their poems to a white magazine, recently two Negro poets declined to submit their poems to a black periodical.[10]

A good introduction to the spectrum of divergent opinions on the Black aesthetic, at an earlier stage of its development in the United States, is the January 1968 issue of *Negro Digest* devoted in large part to a survey of the views of thirty-eight Black writers on black literature today in response to twenty-five questions submitted by the magazine. Most of the writers polled expressed approval, in one form or another, with concepts being developed in the Black aesthetic movement.

There was one interesting difference of approach among the proponents: some of the writers believed that a Black aesthetic is something entirely new that is still to be created, while others maintained that it already exists; that it is embodied in the slave culture and the black people's culture that produced the blues, the spirituals, the folk songs, the

23

work songs and jazz; and that it has to be developed further primarily on the basis of Black folk culture, especially blues and jazz.

Two of the older, established, and widely hailed black poets responded very positively to the Black aesthetic concept in the survey: Gwendolyn Brooks, the only Black writer awarded a Pulitzer Prize, and Margaret Walker, the poet and novelist. Gwendolyn Brooks greeted the Black aesthetic as a most exciting concept because it is "definite," an "entity," and "distinct." Margaret Walker saw the Black aesthetic as a cultural reality with a long historical past going back in time to the beginning of civilization in Egypt, alluding to its African roots and the pre-European flowering of non-Western cultures and civilizations.

The *Negro Digest* survey also disclosed some prominent opponents of the idea of the Black aesthetic. Saunders Redding voiced the view that "aesthetics has no racial, national or geographical boundaries. Beauty and truth, the principal components of aesthetics, are universal." Robert Hayden, the American Negro poet who was awarded the international Grand Prize for Poetry at the First World Festival of Negro Arts in Dakar, Senegal, in 1965, told *Negro Digest*:

> It seems to me that a "black aesthetic" would only be possible in a predominantly black culture. Yet not even black African writers subscribe to such an aesthetic. And isn't the so called "black aesthetic" simply protest and racist propaganda in a new guise?

24

Ralph Ellison is also in disagreement with the theories of the Black aesthetic. His disagreement with the concepts and criteria of negritude as "the reverse of that racism with which prejudiced Whites approached Negroes" (*Harper's Magazine,* March 1967) is well known. Proponents of the Black aesthetic have frequently criticized Ellison not only for what they believe is his aloofness from the Black movements of today, but for what they believe are literary criteria which are too universal, too Western, too divorced from Black criteria.

There are unmistakable differences of literary opinion and theory between Ellison and proponents of the Black aesthetic, but there is one common premise which should not be overlooked: Ellison too, in his own way, rejects "the doctrine of cultural hierarchy" and upholds the unique qualities and style of life which the Black man has developed in America. Ellison's *Invisible Man,* in the epilogue of the novel, reaches the conclusion:

> Now I know men are different and that all life is divided and that only in division is there true health . . . . Whence all this passion toward conformity anyway?—diversity is the word. Let man keep his many parts and you'll have no tyrant states. Why, if they follow this conformity business they'll end up by forcing me, an invisible man, to become white, which is not a color but the lack of one. Must I strive towards colorlessness? But seriously, and without snobbery, think of what the world would lose if that should happen. America is woven of many strands: I would recognize them and let it so remain." [11]

25

In his article in the recent special issue of *Time* devoted to "Black America 1970" Ellison stresses the significance of the unique American Negro style to American culture and life as a whole. He emphasizes the fact that "the timbre of the African voice and the listening habits of the African ear," have had a marked influence on the shaping and development of the American language and describes "the presence of Negro American style" as a very important quality and contribution to America as a whole.[1 2] But Ellison is quite unique among major Black writers in his sense of complete synthesis with Western culture, in his comfortable feeling of belonging undividedly in American literature, and in his disavowal of African origins in his form of expression. The proponents of the Black aesthetic, like their predecessors in the negritude movement in the French-speaking Caribbean, in the West Indies, and in Africa, feel far more acutely the rejection and humiliation of the Black man by the West, the alienation and estrangement of the Black artist in the West.

James Baldwin, in contrast to Ellison's position, declared in "A Letter to Americans" which he published in the journal *Freedomways* (Spring 1968):

> Furthermore, *all* black Americans are born into a society which is determined—repeat: determined—that they shall never learn the truth about themselves or their society, which is determined that black men shall use as their only frame of reference what white Americans convey to them of their own potentialities, and of the share, size, dimensions and possibilities of the world. And I do

not hesitate for an instant to condemn this as a crime. To persuade black boys and girls, as we have for so many generations that their lives are worth less than other lives, and that they can only live on terms dictated to them by other people, by people who despise them, is worse than a crime, it is the sin against the Holy Ghost.

At the First International Conference of Negro Artists and Writers in Paris (1956) Richard Wright observed:

I have spent most of my adult life and most of my waking hours brooding upon the destiny of the race to which I belong by accident of birth and by accident of history . . . . First of all, my position is a split one. I'm black. I'm a man of the West. These hard facts condition, to some degree, my outlook. I see and understand the West; but I also see and understand the non- or anti-Western point of view. How is this possible? This double vision of mine stems from my being a product of Western civilization and from my racial identity which is organically born of my being a product of that civilization. Being a Negro living in a white Western Christian society, I've never been allowed to blend, in a natural and healthy manner, with the culture and civilization of the West. This contradiction of being both Western and a man of color creates a distance, so to speak, between me and my environment . . . . Me and my environment are one, but that oneness has in it, at its very heart, a schism. I regard my position as natural, though others, that is Western whites, would have to make a most strenuous effort of imagination to grasp it . . . .

Since I'm detached from, because of racial conditions, the West, why do I bother to call myself
Western at all? What is it that prompts me to make
an identification with the West despite the contradiction involved? The fact is that I really have no
choice in the matter. Historical forces more powerful than I am have shaped me as a Westerner. I have
not consciously elected to be a Westerner; I have
been made into a Westerner. Long before I had the
freedom to choose I was molded a Westerner. It
began in childhood. And the process continues.

Hence, standing shoulder to shoulder with the
Western white man, speaking his tongue, sharing
his culture, participating in the common efforts of
the Western community, I say to that white man:
"I'm Western, just as Western as you are, maybe
more; but I don't completely agree with you." . . .
My point of view is a Western one, but a Western
one that conflicts at several vital points with the
outlook of the West![13]

It is no accident that Richard Wright made this point at
an international conference of the negritude movement,
before Black writers who belong to different literatures and
cultures, and who are fully as familiar with Western culture as
their white counterparts. But despite differences in immediate backgrounds, their Black experience in the Western
world united them.

During the same conference, a significant debate ensued
between those who spoke of a single African Negro culture
and those who stressed the diversity of African cultures and

the perspective that a variety of national cultures will develop in Africa freed from colonialism.

Leopold Sedar Senghor, the Senegalese intellectual and political leader, also delivered a paper at this conference. He argued that "image and rhythm . . . are the two fundamental features of African Negro style," and thus distinguished between the "African aesthetic," the negritude equivalent of "Black aesthetic," and the European aesthetic. According to Senghor,

> The spirit of African Negro civilization, consciously or not, animates the best Negro artists and writers of today, whether they come from Africa or America." [14]

At this conference the West Indian novelist, George Lamming, also offered some observations on the Black writer in his paper, "The Negro Writer and His World," in which he said:

> To speak of the situation of the Negro writer is to speak, therefore, of a problem of Man, and, more precisely, of a contemporary situation which surrounds us with an urgency that is probably unprecedented. It is to speak, in a sense, of the universal sense of separation and abandonment, frustration and loss, and above else, of some direct inner experience of something missing . . . . There are, I would suggest, three kinds of worlds to which the writer bears in some way a responsibility, worlds which are distinct, and yet very deeply related. There is first of all the world of the private and hidden self . . . . But that private world of the

writer is modified, even made possible, by the
world in which he moves among other men. Much
as he may wish that through, the presence of the
others that one's own presence is given meaning.
What, then, is the relation of a writer to a society
in which, for reasons which have nothing to do
with his work, he is regarded as different? When
that difference carries consequences of injustice,
his relation is not different from that of any other
who shares a similar misfortune. An identical
suffering holds them together in attack or defense
with those who are part of his misfortune; and
since this misfortune of difference enters his
private world, one expects his work as a writer to
be, in part, a witness to that misfortune.[15]

And it was at this conference too that Aimé Césaire, the
Martinican poet, who originally coined the word "negritude,"
proposed the "common denominator" of Black cultures:

We have wondered what is the common denominator of an assembly that can unite men as
different as Africans of native Africa, and North
Americans, as men from the West Indies and from
Madagascar.

To my way of thinking the answer is obvious and
may be briefly stated in the words: colonial
situation. . . . I think it is very true that culture
must be national. It is, however, self-evident that
national cultures, however differentiated they may
be, are grouped by affinities. Moreover, these great
cultural relationships, these great cultural families,
have a name: they are called *civilisations.* In other

words, if it is an undoubted fact that there is a French national culture, an Italian, English, Spanish, German, Russian, etc., national culture, it is no less evident that all these cultures, alongside genuine differences, show a certain number of striking similarities so that, though we can speak of national cultures peculiar to each of the countries mentioned above, we can equally well speak of a European civilisation.

In the same way we can speak of a large family of African cultures which collectively deserve the name of Negro-African culture and which individually reveal the different cultures proper to each country of Africa. And we know that the hazards of history have caused the domain of this civilisation, the locus of this civilisation, to exceed widely the boundaries of Africa. It is in this sense, therefore, that we may say that there are, if not centres, at least fringes of this Negro-African civilisation in Brazil and in the West Indies, in Haiti and the French Antilles and even in the United States. . . .

This is tantamount to saying that civilisation and culture define two aspects of the same thing; civilisation defining the widest outskirts of culture, its most external and most general aspects, while culture represents an internal irradiant cell that is the most unique aspect of a civilisation. . . . Thus, all culture is specific. Specific in that it is the work of a single particular will, choosing between different possibilities. . . .

All who have met here are united by a double solidarity; on the one hand, a *horizontal solidarity,* that is, a solidarity created for us by the colonial, semi-colonial or para-colonial situation imposed upon us from without; and on the other, a vertical solidarity, a *solidarity in time,* due to the fact that we started from an original unity, the unity of African civilisation, which has become diversified into a whole series of cultures all of which, in varying degrees, owe something to that civilisation. [16]

Here, in his own personal way and style but incorporating the theoretical contributions of the Haitian scholar Dr. Jean Price-Mars, who illuminated the transatlatic African survivals and the dynamism of Negro cultures in the Americas, and ideas that evolved out of two decades or so of negritude movement thinking, Césaire proclaimed the theoretical conceptions later incorporated in the Second Congress of Negro Writers and Artists which met in Rome in 1959. The slogan of this Second Congress was "The Unity of Negro African Cultures." This congress, like the first conference of 1956, was organized by the Society of African Culture and *Présence Africaine,* the magazine of the negritude movement which was established in Paris in 1947 and remains very much alive today.

The birth of the movement preceded the magazine, as *Présence Africaine* repeatedly reminds its readers in these words:

Since 1941 Africans, Madagascans, and West Indians in Paris have been preoccupied with affirming the "presence" of ethos of the black communities of the world, of defending the originality of their way of life and the dignity of their cultures.[17]

Alioune Diop, the Senegalese intellectual who founded *Présence Africaine,* declared in the opening speech of the Second Congress in 1959:

One of our tasks is imposed by the need for our peoples to escape assimilation, to de-westernise themselves so as not to stifle their own genius. This de-westernising tendency, readily observable in our countries, from Madagascar to Haiti, from Timbuctoo to Johannesburg, from Nigeria to Kenya, is aimed both at institutions, hierarchies and authorities, and at means of expression, ethical references and historical values. We are determined to retain the gifts of the West, on condition that they are used according to our own genius and our own circumstances, ... That is why, reasonably and legitimately, we take as our mission to work, each in his own field, toward freeing the mental disciplines and the arts from those shackles with which the compromised demands of Western hegemony have their universal application. To de-westernise in order to universalise, such is our desire. To universalise, it is necessary that all should participate in the creative work of mankind .... Our artists and our writers intend therefore to use a language, a type of aesthetics perceptibly different from those of the West.[18]

The Black aesthetic therefore has roots in an older international tradition which has long been combating white racism and defining the distinctiveness of Black cultures. In the United States, Blacks were hopeful that their earlier cultural movements would flourish within an integrated society based on cultural pluralism and diversity. But before today's angry Black American poets appeared on the scene, earlier Black poets in the Caribbean had rejected this very notion of assimilation. Thus, Aimé Céssaire in one of his *Soleil cou-coupe* poems exclaimed:

Europe
I give my support to all that powders the sky with
      its insolence
to all that is loyal and fraternal to all that has the
      courage to be eternally
new to all that can give its heart to fire to all that
      has the strength to
burst from an inexhaustible sap to all that is calm
      and sure
to all that is not you
Europe
pompous name for excrement [19]

Or, according to Leon Damas (Guiana),

I feel ridiculous
in their shoes, in their dress suits,
in their starched shirts, in their hard collars,
in their monocles and bowler hats.

And farther on he observes:

I feel ridiculous
with their theories which they season
according to their needs and their passions.

I feel ridiculous
among them, an accomplice, among them a pimp,
among them a murderer, my hands terrifyingly red
with the blood of their civilisation.[20]

Frantz Fanon, who questioned some aspects of the negritude movement declared at the Second Congress of Negro Writers and Artists in 1959, that Western racism is the cause of this anti-Western attitude:

The Negro, never so much a Negro as since he has been dominated by the whites, when he decides to prove that he has a culture and to behave like a cultured person, comes to realize that history points out a well-defined path to him: he must demonstrate that a Negro culture exists.

And it is only too true that those who are most responsible for this racialization of thought, or at least for the first movement toward that thought, are and remain those Europeans who have never ceased to set up white culture to fill the gap left by the absence of other cultures. Colonialism did not dream of wasting its time in denying the existence of one national culture after another. The concept of negritude, for example, was the emotional if not the logical antithesis of that insult which the white man flung at humanity. This rush of negritude against the white man's contempt showed itself in certain spheres to be the one idea capable of lifting interdictions and anathemas. . . . The Negroes who live in the United States and in Central or Latin America in fact experience the need to attach themselves to a cultural matrix. Their problem is not fundamentally different from that of the Africans. The whites of America did not mete out to them any different treatment from that of the whites who ruled over the Africans. We have seen that the whites were used to putting all Negroes in the same bag. [21]

Fanon believed that a diversity of national cultures would evolve in Africa, rather than a "black culture," and he stressed that "the essential problems" confronting the American Negroes "were not the same as those that confronted the African Negroes." In this same paper, in which he criticized the limitations of negritude, as he saw them, he also noted that American Negroes "of their own accord" were considering "their problems from the same standpoint as those of their African brothers," and he stressed that negritude was a reaction to the White racist contempt for Black people and their cultures universally, in all countries in which Black people live. [22]

The Black aesthetic movement in the U.S. has developed from the fundamental antiracism of negritude. Many African writers, notably the prominent Nigerian writers Wole Soyinka and Chinhua Achebe, and the South African writer in exile Ezekiel Mphahlele, have long been engaged in public disagreement with various basic tenets of the old negritude, particularly with the mystique and concepts of Senghor. Mphahlele, writing from his perspective of a multiracial African society in South Africa, has counterposed to negritude and Senghor's views, the idea of three hundred years of "cultural cross breeding," of "unconsciously taking and throwing away and sifting" which have resulted in a distinctive South African content and form particularly in choral and jazz music, indicating "a merging of cultures."[23] Soyinka and Achebe have addressed themselves to the new problems of the African writer after the defeat of direct colonial rule and the birth of independent African states: the struggle for artistic freedom against the imposition of literary doctrines and programs, negritudinal or not, by the state, and the struggle for the individual vision and integrity of the artist.

Wole Soyinka has outlined three stages experienced by African writers now living in independent states. First, "united opposition by the colonised to the external tyrant." Then "with few exceptions the writer directed his energies to enshrining victory, to re-affirming his identification with the aspirations of nationalism and the stabilisation of society." In 1967, in an article in *Transition* and in his speech at the African-Scandinavian Writers' Conference in Stockholm, he spoke of a third and present stage, "the stage of disillusionment," and declared:

> In new societies which begin the seductive experiment in authoritarianism, it has become a familiar experience to watch society crush the writer under a load of guilt for his daring to express a sensibility and an outlook apart from, and independent of, the mass direction. [24]

And Soyinka stressed that this is not at all a singularly African phenomenon but something global, "the recurrent cycle of human stupidity." [25]

Chinhua Achebe, in an article published in 1966, wrote:

A new situation has thus arisen. One of the writer's main functions has always been to expose and attack injustice. Should we keep at the old theme of racial injustice (sore as it still is) when new injustices have sprouted all around us? I think not . . . . The black writer in independent Africa is thus facing his first real challenge. Will he accept it? He will be told many good reasons why he should not: it would be treacherous to the African revolution; it would supply ammunition to the enemies of his race . . . . We must seek the freedom to express our thought and feeling, even against ourselves, without the anxiety that what we say might be taken in evidence against our race. We have stood in the dock too long pleading and protesting before ruffians and frauds masquerading as disinterested judges. [26]

For years we have been reading postmortems on negritude, partly because of the sharp criticism of many of its tenets by African writers and Black writers in the West, but the postmortems have repeatedly proved to be premature. The strong current of antiracist feeling and thinking in negritude will not disappear or die so long as White racism exists. The new wave of negritude in the Black aesthetic movement in the U.S.—unprecedented in intensity and scope—is evidence of the stubborn persistence of racism in our country, of the movement toward "two societies, one Black, one white—separate and unequal" about which the 1968 Kerner Commission Report warned, of the failures of integration and desegregation.

The general American literary periodicals have paid limited attention to the Black aesthetic. They tend to equate it with the single anthology *Black Fire*, which is only one expression of a diverse movement. A review article by Jack Richardson in *The New York Review* (December 19, 1968) actually suggests that "madness" is "a reasonably accurate descriptive term for much of what is happening in Negro literature and in the criticism surrounding it." But in fact, the negritude and Black aesthetic movements have raised fundamental questions about the failures of Western literary criticism and literary theory.

Modern literary criticism has focused much of its attention on the intrinsic qualities and cohesive structures of literary works and the decisive importance of the personal imagination in artistic creation, but it has not rejected the significance of an author's connections with a larger group of people and with a particular environment and historical development. Modern literary theory accepts and works with the concepts of national literature and regional literature, difficult as it is to define with precision how the individual imagination of the artist gives expression to his nationality or his regional environment or the spirit of a people.

Northrop Frye has shown that "every form in literature has a pedigree, and we can trace its descent back to the earliest times."[27] Frye has done this for Western literary forms, and Black writers and scholars are examining the African pedigrees of Black forms of expression as well as the African elements in cultural interaction with Western forms.

Comparative literature has devoted much attention to Western national literatures, and to the historical community of national writings which form the basic unity of Western literature. But Western literary criticism has not come to terms in any recognized or satisfactory way with the far more complex question of ethnic writing generally, particularly the historical community of the literatures of Africa and Blacks in the West.

As literary scholars, I think it is our duty to recognize how Western criticism has failed in this important area of study. We have to begin paying serious attention to the challenges advanced by the negritude and Black aesthetic movements and seriously studying the theoretical contributions already made by Black writers and scholars. We cannot just sweep under the rug the serious criticism by Black and White scholars that in Western culture the concept of the universal has so frequently been distorted into a Procrustean bed against non-Western cultures and into a norm of White Western superiority. It is the duty of literary scholars to examine fully the racist influences on Western concepts of the universal and to correct racist distortions with the understanding that the universal means being receptive to, and consciously welcoming, the diverse cultures and diverse aesthetic creations of Black people of the world for the cultural enrichment of humanity.

NOTES

1. W. E. Burghardt DuBois, *The Souls of Black Folk* (Greenwich, Conn.: Crest Reprint, 1964), p. 185.

2. Hoyt W. Fuller, "A Survey: Black Writers Views on Literary Lions and Values," *Negro Digest* 17, no. 3 (January 1968): 10.

3. Frantz Fanon, *Toward the African Revolution (Political Essays)* (New York: Grove Press, 1969), p. 31.

4. David Hume, *The Philosophical Works*, (1882: reprint, Darmstadt, Germany: Scientia Verlag Aalen, 1964), III, 252.

5. *The Black Prince, A True Story; Being An Account of the Life and Death of Naimbana, An African King's Son, etc.* (Philadelphia B. & J. Johnson, 1800), pp. 11-13.

6. LeRoi Jones, "The Legacy of Malcolm X, and the Coming of the Black Nation." In *Home: Social Essays* (New York: William Morrow & Co., 1966), pp. 247-248.

7. Hoyt W. Fuller, "Towards a Black Aesthetic." In *Black Expression: Essays by and About Black Americans in the Creative Arts,* edited by Addison Gayle, Jr. (New York: Weybright and Talley, 1969), pp. 266-267, 269.

8. Hoyt W. Fuller, "Introduction Toward the Black Aesthetic," *Nommo 1,* no. 1 (1969): 3.

9. James T. Stewart, "The Development of the Black Revolutionary Artist." In *Black Fire: An Anthology of Afro-American Writing,* edited by LeRoi Jones and Larry Neal (New York: William Morrow & Co., 1968), pp. 3, 6.

10. Dudley Randall, "Black Poetry." In *Black Expression*, edited by Addison Gayle, Jr. (New York: Weybright and Talley, 1969), pp. 109-114.

11. Ralph Ellison, *Invisible Man* (New York: Signet, 1963), p. 499.

12. Ralph Ellison, "What America Would Be Like Without Blacks," *Time,* 6 April 1970, p. 55.

13. Richard Wright, "Tradition and Industrialization," *Présence Africaine,* no. 8-9-10 (November 1956): 356-360. This special triple issue of the journal published the proceedings of the First International Conference of Negro Writers and Artists (Paris, September 19-22, 1956) and is hereafter cited as 1956 Conference Proceedings.

14. L. S. Senghor, "The Spirit of Civilisation, or The Laws of African Negro Culture," *Présence Africaine,* 1956 Conference Proceedings, 58 and 68.

15. George Lamming, "The Negro Writer and His World," *Présence Africaine,* 1956 Conference Proceedings, pp. 329, 330, 331.

16. Aimé Césaire, "Culture and Colonisation," *Présence Africaine,* 1956 Conference Proceedings, pp. 193-195.

17. *Présence Africaine,* 1956 Conference Proceedings, supplement of advertisements, p. 1.

18. Alioune Diop, "The Meaning of This Congress," *Présence Africaine,* no. 24-25 (February-May 1959): 49-52.

19. G. R. Coulthard, *Race and Color in Caribbean Literature* (London: Oxford Univ. Press, 1962), p. 45.

20. Ibid., pp. 44-45.

21. Frantz Fanon, *The Wretched of the Earth* (New York: Grove Press, 1968), pp. 212, 215.

22. Ibid., pp. 234, 216, 215.

23. Ezekiel Mphahlele, *The African Image* (New York: Praeger, 1962), p. 28.

24. Wole Soyinka, "The Writer in a Modern African State." In *The Writer in Modern Africa: African-Scandinavian Writers' Conference, Stockholm 1967,* edited by Per Wästberg (New York: Africana Publishing Corporation, 1969), pp. 16, 15.

25. Ibid, p. 20.

26. Chinua Achebe, "The Black Writer's Burden," *Présence Africaine* 31, no. 59 (1966): 138-139.

27. Northrop Frye, *The Educated Imagination* (Bloomington: Indiana Univ. Press, 1964), p. 40.

BLACK LITERATURE AND THE PROBLEM OF EVALUATION

Nick Aaron Ford

The case for Black literature in the curricula of American schools and colleges has won a sympathetic hearing in all sections of the nation, but its effective implementation has been hampered by troublesome problems whose solutions depend upon a greater willingness and determination to alter fundamentally certain deeply rooted attitudes and thought patterns that have produced the current dilemma. Signs of such alterations, however, are not yet visible. One problem is the lack of a meaningful definition of terms. Another is the inability to recruit and train qualified teachers. A third is the failure of administrations, faculties,

45

and students to agree upon a satisfactory organizational pattern in which the subject matter can best be presented. The chief concern of this paper is the problem of evaluation.

Before proceeding further, let us consider some definitions of terms used in this paper. By *Black* literature I mean literature concerning "the Black experience" by Black writers of African ancestry who have spent most of their lives in the United States. By *literature* I mean writing designed primarily for pleasure or contemplation rather than for the presentation of facts for their own sake. The *American College Dictionary* defines *evaluate* as "to ascertain the value...of; appraise carefully." Value is defined as "that property of a thing because of which it is esteemed, desirable, or useful...; worth, merit, or importance." I accept these dictionary definitions as the bases for my use of the term *evaluation.*

I am acutely aware that *literary evaluation* in this contemporary period is an unpopular concept and that critics who do not wish to place their reputations in jeopardy generally avoid the subject. Emil Staiger suggests, "Every genuine writer, and every reader endowed with some sense of artistic quality, will react to the problem of literary evaluation with intense suspicion."[1] René Wellek, author of the five-volume *History of Modern Criticism,* after condemning recent attempts of some scholars to doubt the whole enterprise of literary theory and to absorb all literary study into history, admits that "any criticism is today on the defensive." There are, of course, distinguished scholars who object to contemporary discussions of literary evaluation not because they are not concerned about values but because for them the case for literary values was settled long ago, and it was settled on the basis of one criterion only: the criterion of aestheticism. Others object because they insist that literary evaluation is completely personal and a discussion of general approaches or methods is futile. Still other objections are based on the premise that literature is primarily a report on human experience and that no one has the right to downgrade the value of any human experience.

Despite arguments to the contrary, I believe a satisfactory solution to the problem of evaluation in relation to the effective inclusion of Black literature in school and college curricula is crucial. My conclusion is based on the following considerations:

1. Although there may be no public acknowledgment of the involvement of critical standards or guidelines in the selection of literary works for study in English classes, there can be no doubt of such involvement. The mere selection of anthologies to be used in literature classes, as well as the choice of specific works from the adopted anthology, implies the use of the process of evaluation. Since this sub-terranean process has, with few exceptions, completely ignored from the beginning of American education to the present the whole corpus of Black literature (excluding literature by Whites about Blacks which my definition does not cover), it is necessary that these time-worn prejudicial bases for evaluation be openly acknowledged and reexamined for the purpose of making fundamental revisions that will include the newly discovered dimensions of Black literature.

2. Failure to provide revised approaches to evaluation will justify the current demand of some groups for completely separate modes of evaluation for the selection and study of Black literature. Such a development would tend to destroy the concept of literature as a legitimate subdivision of humanistic study with common principles of organization of and insight into the human experience which distinguish it from history, philosophy, and sociology. Under such conditions either Black literature or non-Black literature as now defined would deserve a new nomenclature.

3. If Black literature is to be included in school and college curricula, teachers must be available to teach it. Yet, some Black students, teachers, and critics say that White teachers cannot teach and White critics cannot evaluate Black literature. Since there are many Black teachers who say they are no more qualified to teach it than their White colleagues, it appears that the subject will never be widely taught until the majority of English teachers are prepared to teach it and Black students are prepared to acknowledge the ability of qualified White instructors to teach it. I believe that if acceptable approaches to evaluation are developed and generally agreed upon by scholars and critics, there will be no legitimate reason for demanding color as the test for competent teachers of the subject. My experience in working with White teachers on the high school and college levels who now teach Black literature, or are planning to do so, have convinced me that their

competency would be greatly enhanced and their self-doubts largely dissipated if the problem of literary evaluation could be satisfactorily solved.

4. The insistence upon a reappraisal of critical standards in the hope of broadening the definition of literature to include the Black variety could also serve to recognize officially the present tacit approval of such new trends as Truman Capote's *In Cold Blood,* Norman Mailer's *Armies of the Night,* and perhaps Philip Roth's *Portnoy's Complaint.*

A glance backward over the history of criticism reveals that there are only four major types of criteria for literary evaluation. The first, advocated by Plato and his numerous adherents, is the capacity of the work to produce moral or political good. The second, originating with Aristotle and embraced by a multitude of followers, is the author's ability to impose upon or discover in nature or experience an ideal pattern that makes sense within the limits and conditions set by the writer. The third, formulated by Benedetto Croce although indebted to Aristotelian philosophy, is the extent to and effectiveness with which the literary work accomplishes the intention of the author. The fourth, which owes its popularity to the so-called "new critics," rests upon the author's achievement of technical competence as manifested in such qualities as complexity, compression, tension, irony, symbolism, and so on, qualities that are supposed to enhance aesthetic pleasure. For the purposes of this limited discussion I have felt the necessity to summarize in a small number of general categories the abundant proliferations of critical dogma, but it must be clearly understood that each category represents variations in statement and application too numerous to delineate. Although these criteria have competed with each other from time to time for privileged position, since the Romantic period at least none has won unconditional acceptance.

Now that I have, in this brief introduction, presented arguments to support my contentions that literary evaluation is an unsolved problem, that there is a wide variety of conflicting attitudes in the scholarly community concerning its nature and proper aims, and that a satisfactory resolution of the problem resulting in general agreement upon common goals acceptable to presently divergent groups is necessary to the successful inclusion of Black literature in school and college curricula, let us turn to an examination of my proposed solution.

I propose that all literary scholars and critics actively engaged in their professions seriously consider, individually and collectively, the urgent need to revise drastically traditional norms for evaluating literature according to the WASP pattern in order to include such variations as explorations of the Black experience by Black writers, as well as the experiences of other ethnic minorities by their own indigenous writers. To deny that a narrow, prejudiced pattern of evaluation has existed in the past, and does still exist, is to compound error with self-righteousness and arrogance and to invite the complete rejection of school and college literature by the brightest and most sensitive youths of this generation.

John H. Fisher, executive secretary of the Modern Language Association, recognized this threat when he recently stated,

> The subject of English in this country has been used to inculcate a white, Anglo-Saxon, Protestant ethic. This was our principal and most valuable inheritance from the mother country. The most important people in "English" in this country have traditionally been whose who outdid the British at their own game—did better scholarship on Chaucer, Shakespeare, or Milton; brought over the most English books to found a Folger or a Huntington, or a University of Illinois library. . .[2]

Robert F. Hogan, executive secretary of the National Council of Teachers of English, acknowledged a similar anxiety about the growing irrelevance of school and college literature when he said,

> The question is whether the teachers—school and college—who "profess" English want to occupy the central position they now maintain, or whether they will be content to move toward peripheral positions analogous to those occupied by Latin and Greek in the schools, or to the one occupied by Classics in many colleges and universities. It is well and good to argue that central to our responsibility is giving our students, at whatever level, access to the best that man has thought and said. A basic thought is, "How many are listening to what *we* have selected as the best that man has thought or said?" The answer has to be, "Not very many."[3]

Recently the well known scholar and critic, Alfred Kazin, in a lecture at Barat College, admitted that aging professors like himself are "living through the valley of the shadow" because their students no longer care about the *tradition* of literature as those professors have been accustomed to think of it. "But the fact is," he confesses,

> We are seeing an understandable revolt against literature itself. Literature is no longer the queen of the arts. There are just too many other forms of artistic expression, whether in film or in rock or whatever. The whole idea of literature was so much bound up with solitude. One man sitting in a room looking at a white paper, slowly and painfully pushing his thoughts along—this no longer seems possible in the insanely over-populated and gregarious society in which we live, where one is aware all the time of such human struggles and aspirations and despairs that we can no longer imagine saying, as Joyce did, that the artist should be like God in the creation, present everywhere and visible nowhere.[4]

Several years ago Yale University's distinguished historian, C. Van Woodward president of the American Historical Association, challenged the scholars in his profession to address themselves to a similar problem by ending the South-oriented writing and teaching of American history, particularly in relation to the Negro.

I suggest that the following shifts in emphases will greatly contribute to the realization of my proposal.

52

First, the overwhelming insistence upon aestheticism as the major criterion for literary evaluation must be repudiated. Aestheticism, which concerns us here, is defined in *The American College Dictionary* aas follows: 1. *the acceptance of artistic beauty and taste as a fundamental standard, ethical and other standards being secondary. 2. an exaggerated devotion to art, music, or poetry, with indifference to practical matters.* I charge that this kind of aestheticism has been the guiding principle of literary evaluation by American scholars and critics at least since the advent of the "new criticism" more than thirty years ago, and that if it continues to dominate, there can be no alternative to the demands of the Black revolutionists for completely separate standards of evaluation for Black literature.

In a significant sense the emphasis on aestheticism is an emphasis on the formal, the nonhuman, the determination not to become involved in the sordid aspect of the human condition, the preoccupation with contemplating the stars while bogging down in the muck and mire of the terrestial terrain. It may be more than a coincidence that aestheticism enjoyed its greatest veneration in a period when the unimaginable horrors of the atomic bomb were inflicted upon the unsuspecting civilians of Hiroshima and Nagasaki. If Kipling was right in his prophecy,

> By all ye cry or whisper,
> By all ye leave or do,
> The silent sullen peoples
> Shall weigh your Gods and you

those silent sullen students forced to sit under the tutelage of English professors committed completely to the theory of aestheticism are now giving short weight to the professor's "god" and less than serious attention to the professor himself.

At its worst the glorification of aestheticism can mean the false belief that literature exists in a vacuum or is the special property of aristocrats with extraordinary sensibilities. Commenting on the philosophic tenets of the American apostles of the "new criticism," Alfred Kazin charges, in *On Native Grounds*, that

> on the obvious level this criticism resulted in a literature of aestheticism that was a defense against modern life. . . . Underneath all the trappings of neoclassic snobbery and the obsession with form as an ideal end in itself, it was a profound and impotent disaffection that moved in this criticism.[5]

He quotes John Crowe Ransom's insistence that the modern poet is above the sentimental glorification of poetry as a guide of life, though the modern reader has as yet "no recognition of the possibility that an asthetic effect may exist by itself, independent of morality or any other useful set of ideals."[6]

Concerning Allen Tate, who occupies a place among the hierarchy of aesthetic critics equal if not superior to that of Ransom, Kazin says

> What one saw in Tate's system was a fantastic inversion of the Marxist system. . . . The Marxist

critic could study a work of art only in terms of its social relations; Tate would study literature—that is, only poetry of a certain intensity and difficulty—precisely because it had no social relations at all. . . . Tate never admitted specific formal properties of literature and its relation to civilization.[7]

In *Reactionary Essays* Tate gave himself away most completely when he wrote that while slavery was wrong, it was wrong because the master gave everything to the slave and got nothing in return, that the "moral" wrong of slavery meant nothing since "societies can bear an amazing amount of corruption and still produce high cultures."[8]

Is it any wonder that a theory of evaluation with a history and operating principles such as the one characterized above can never acknowledge Black literature as a legitimate part of the literary spectrum? Is it any wonder that those who are genuinely concerned about securing equal consideration for the place of Black literature in American studies must demand the repudiation of aestheticism as the most privileged criterion for literary evaluation?

In an article discussing the current "Black Arts Movement," Larry Neal, Black poet and critic, explains how Black literature differs in aims and methods from the standards of White-Anglo-Saxon-Protestant aestheticism:

It is radically opposed to any concept of the artist that alienates him from his community. Black art is the aesthetic and spiritual sister of the Black Power concept. As such it envisions an art that speaks directly to the ˌneeds and aspirations of Black

55

America. In order to perform this task, the Black
Arts Movement proposes a radical reordering of the
western cultural aesthetic. It proposes a separate
symbolism, mythology, and iconology. . . . The
two movements postulate that there are in fact and
in spirit two Americas—one black, one white. It is
the opinion of many Black writers. . .that the
western aesthetic has run its course: it is impossible
to construct anything meaningful written in its
decaying structure.[9]

Although I do not subscribe to all of Neal's fears and
dire predictions as of this moment, all available evidence
points to the conclusion that unless the literary establishment
takes seriously the need for a reordering of evaluative
standards and procedures *now*, without further subterfuge,
many of us who still believe in the "humanity" of our
discipline and those who practice it will be forced to
acknowledge, like Cardinal Wolsey, a great betrayal. An
example of the current travesty of literary evaluation on the
basis of aestheticism insofar as Black literature is concerned
can be seen in the ridiculous naiveté of Allen Tate in his
Preface to Melvin Tolson's *Libretto for the Republic of
Liberia.*

The Republic of Liberia, Africa, founded in 1847,
commissioned Melvin B. Tolson, a Black American poet to
write a poem in honor of the centennial. Tolson's first
volume of poems, *Rendezvous With America* (1944), had
demonstrated worthy poetic talent. In fulfillment of the
terms of his commission, he wrote a long commemorative
poem published in 1953 entitled *Libretto for the Republic of*

Africa. In a Preface to the volume, Allen Tate said, among other things equally as naive:

> For the first time, it seems to me, a Negro poet has assimilated completely the full poetic language of his time and, by implication, the language of the Anglo-American tradition. I do not wish to be understood as saying that Negro poets have hither-to been incapable of this assimilation; there has been perhaps rather a resistance to it on the part of those Negroes who supposed that their peculiar genius lay in "folk" idiom or in the romantic creation of a "new" language within the English language. In these directions interesting and even distinguished work has been done, notably by Langston Hughes and Gwendolyn Brooks. But there are two disadvantages to this approach: first, the "folk" and "new" languages are not very different from those that white poets can write; secondly, the distinguishing Negro quality is not in the language but in the subject-matter, which is usually the plight of the Negro in a White culture. The plight is real and often tragic; but I cannot think that, *from the literary point of view,* the tragic aggressiveness of the modern Negro poet offers wider poetic possibilities than the resigned pathos of Paul Lawrence Dunbar, who was only a "White" *poéte manqué.* Both attitudes have limited the Negro poet to a provincial mediocrity in which one's feelings about one's difficulties become more important than poetry itself.

> It seems to me only common sense to assume that the main thing is the poetry, if one is a poet, whatever one's color may be. I think Mr. Tolson

has assumed this; and the assumption, I gather, has made him not less but more intensely *Negro* in his apprehension of the world than any of his contemporaries, or any that I have read.[10]

I have been content to use the word naiveté in respect to Tate's critical pronouncements in lieu of harsher words such as obtuseness or hypocrisy because it connotes the lesser offense from a critical standpoint. I do not agree with those who say that no White critic is capable of evaluating a literary work by a Black writer simply because he has not lived through the Black experience. Naturally, such a critic cannot give a perfect evaluation, but neither can any critic give a perfect evaluation of any work. I require only that a White critic approach the evaluation of Black literature in the spirit of humility rather than arrogance and only after he has devoted a similar amount of time and careful study to the whole corpus of Black writing as he would normally spend in trying to understand any other unfamiliar field of study. Unfortunately, Tate, like the vast majority of White critics, has not done his homework.

Let us see how uninformed and patently false the evaluation which I have cited is. First, the critic says, "For the first time, it seems to me, a Negro poet has assimilated completely the full poetic language of his time and, by implication, the language of the Anglo-American tradition." The facts are that throughout the whole history of American literature the major criticism of Black writers from Phillis Wheatley (1773) to Gwendolyn Brooks, who was awarded the Pulitzer Prize in 1950, has been that their poetry is the language of the White Anglo-American poetic tradition. Countee Cullen, an acknowledged apostle of John Keats' cult of beauty in language and sentiment, penned a bitter complaint about such critical treatment which ended with the well known lines: "Yet do I marvel at this curious thing. To make a poet black and bid him sing." Paul Laurence Dunbar approximately fifty years earlier, whom Tate accused of "resigned pathos" for his use of the "folk" idiom of Negro dialect, angrily indicted the literary establishment (White publishers, critics, and readers) for ignoring his poems in literary English and praising only those written "in a worn-out tongue." Although Tate ascribes the "mediocrity" of Negro poetry to the Black poet's false supposition that "their peculiar genius lay in 'folk' idiom or in the romantic creation of a 'new' language within the English language," he says some interesting and even distinguished work has been done in this vein, "notably by Langston Hughes and Gwendolyn Brooks." It is a sad commentary on the state of "White-Anglo-Saxon-Protestant criticism in America when a prestigious member of that establishment does not know that scores of Black writers of poetry over a period of two hundred years have assimilated "the language of the Anglo-American tradition" as well as, and in some cases better than, M. B. Tolson's demonstration in 1953.

Furthermore, our critic asserts with evident seriousness that Tolson's assimilation of the language and spirit of the Anglo-American poetic tradition as demonstrated in *Libretto for the Republic of Liberia* "has made him not less but more intensely *Negro* in his apprehension of the world than any of

59

his contemporaries." He makes this judgment despite the fact
that the poet himself has felt it necessary to append his
twenty-nine-page poem, supposedly written in Anglo-
American English with no Negro idioms and very few African
phrases, sixteen pages of notes attempting to clarify his
meanings which he was unable to do in the poem itself and
which with few exceptions have no roots in Black culture.

I hesitate to prolong this agony, but in order to
illustrate how errors by one prominent critic can be passed
on by lesser breeds and even compounded in the process, let
me cite one such example. Selden Rodman, editor of more
than one literary anthology, in his review of Tolson's poem
for *The New York Times Book Review* (January 24, 1954),
endorsed with enthusiasm Tate's Preface and added the
following evaluation.

> It is a reflection on so-called "white" culture that
> up to now "Negro poetry" in English has had to be
> considered as such and handled with special care to
> avoid giving offense. Praised for its moral inten-
> tions and excused for its formal shortcomings, it
> has generally been tolerated as a literary poor
> relation. The fact of the matter is that most of this
> poetry has been second rate, and that critics,
> partaking of the general responsibility for the
> Negro's unreadiness to take the "Negro problem"
> in his stride, have hesitated to say so. . . .
>
> The publication of this extraordinary poem by M.
> B. Tolson. . .bids fair to put an end to all that . . . .
> It is not only by all odds the most considerable
> poem so far written by an American Negro, but a

work of poetic synthesis in the symbolic vein altogether worthy to be discussed in the company of such poems as "The Wasteland," "The Bridge," and "Patterson."

Then turning to the weaknesses of this "best" of all Negro poems, Rodman continues:

This kind of writing becomes at its best academic and at its worst intellectual exhibitionism, throwing at the reader undigested scraps of everything from Bantu to Esperanto in unrelaxed cacophony. Eliot's taste was equal to giving the results of such a method dignity; Tolson's taste is much more uneven.

Although poetry by its very nature suffers most from the application of the canons of aestheticism, the novel has not entirely escaped a similar fate, especially the Black variety when being judged by the White critic. Despite the fact that the most significant novels that are still remembered from past ages have dealt with moral and social issues which confront civilized man, any novel by a Black writer which deals honestly and effectively with the problems of race without attempting to blunt the cutting edge by sublimating it into the larger context of universality is denied serious critical attention in obedience to the strictures of aestheticism. Examples of this treatment can be seen in the critical pronouncements of Robert Bone, author of *The Negro Novel in America,* and generally accepted by White professors as the most respected authority on the subject. Although Bone deserves credit for his pioneering work in the field when

61

other White scholars considered such research beneath
contempt, and although he has furnished some important
new and valid insights in the study of Black novelists, he has
succumbed in much of his evaluation to the fallacy of
aestheticism. At the end of his Epilogue, he declares,

> In exceptional circumstances, then, both the pro-
> test novel and the novel of white life are legitimate
> concerns of the Negro novelist. To restore per-
> spective, however, it is necessary to restate the
> general rule: a high protest content is not likely to
> produce good fiction. . . . He concludes by assuring
> the reader that notable progress is being made as
> more of the younger [Negro] writers have learned
> to respect the difference between social contro-
> versy and art. In the long run an art-centered Negro
> fiction will evolve, free from the crude nationalistic
> propaganda of the past and the subtler assimila-
> tionist propaganda of the present. [11]

Of course, when one condemns the propaganda or
protest novel, or places one below the other in the scale of
his values, much can depend on the definition of terms.
According to my definition of propaganda, the term not only
includes the protest novel but the political, the antiwar, the
religious, and any other kind of novel that fights for or
against a cause. I, therefore, classify as propagandistic
practically all of the novels of Charles Dickens, Sinclair Lewis
(Nobel Prize winner), and Norman Mailer, as well as Dreiser's
An American Tragedy, Hemingway's *A Farewell to Arms,*
and Steinbeck's *The Grapes of Wrath.* However, since none of
these is directed at the problem of race, Bone and most of

the Protestant-Anglo-Saxon oriented critics would disagree. It is this determination to label as propaganda all literary works protesting racism that evidently impelled Bone to evaluate Zora Neal Hurston's *Their Eyes Were Watching God,* reportedly written in seven weeks under the emotional pressure of a recent love affair, as "possibly the best novel of the period (1930-40), excepting *Native Son.*"[12] Such a judgment is amazing when one remembers that Arna Bontemps' magnificent *Black Thunder,* an historical novel about an American slave revolt, was published the previous year, a novel that by all fair standards must be considered less propagandistic than William Styron's *The Confessions of Nat Turner,* which adheres more to the superficialities of aestheticism and less to historical and cultural authenticity.

To keep the record straight, let me emphasize that I am not advocating the complete rejection of aestheticism as *one* of the criteria for literary evaluation. I am rejecting it as *the privileged* or principal criterion for such evaluation. If anywone wants to know what privileged criterion I recommend to replace it, I reply, "none"! I suggest that the time has come to deny any *one* standard a privileged place on the scale of literary evaluation. I agree with Donald Hall in his Introduction to the anthology, *Contemporary American Poetry,* when he says,

> In modern art anarchy has proved preferable to the restrictions of a benevolent tyranny. It is preferable as a permanent condition. We do not want merely to substitute one orthodoxy for another

Nick Aaron Ford

> ... but we want all possibilities, even contra-
> dictory ones, to exist together. The trouble with
> orthodoxy is that it prescribes the thinkable limits
> of variation ... yet typically the modern artist has
> allowed nothing to be beyond his consideration.
> He has acted as if restlessness were a conviction
> and has destroyed his own past in order to create a
> future.[13]

I recommend that one of the criteria for the new catholicity of evaluation be a greater willingness to accept uncensored experience as valuable. Many critics admit that value judgments about events, persons, and artistic creations tell us as much about the evaluators as they do about the thing being evaluated. The greater the range of consciousness the evaluator has achieved, either by actual experience or by a wide variety of reading, the fairer and more objective his evaluation will be. Only by exposure to a diversity of experiences, actual or vicarious, can a reader or critic acquire sufficient background to evaluate without narrow prejudice a new encounter. No critic, scholar, or reader who wishes to have his evaluations taken seriously can refuse to read any serious literary work simply because its language or style or content is offensive to his taste. For his capacity to evaluate any book is diminished by the extent that his experiences with different kinds of books have been limited. Thus a teacher who refuses to consider for use in the bibliography of his course a book dealing honestly but _exclusively_ with the Black experience without conscious or overt overtones of universality is deliberately rejecting _uncensored experience_ as a legitimate criterion for literary evaluation.

64

In my opinion the test of *human values* is another criterion worthy of a high place on the scale of literary evaluation. It is an undeniable fact that literature is written by human beings for human beings. Consequently, one legitimate test of its success must be the extent and degree to which it responds to human needs. The range of human needs is extensive, including the desire for simple entertainment, for fantasy, for myth, for exciting adventure, for Aristotelian catharsis, and for vicarious experiences in alien cultures and religions. Satisfaction of these needs creates the human values of which we speak, values that on the lower levels may be classified as material, factual, or emotional, and on the higher levels intellectual, aesthetic, moral, or spiritual. Thus a blues poem or a vignette from Langston Hughes's *Simple Speaks His Mind*, or a play such as LeRoi Jones's *The Slave Ship* may have little aesthetic value but may be extremely rich in other human values.

Furthermore, I contend that the test of *relevance* must be another criterion for the evaluation of literature of our time. Unless it is so accepted there is little hope that the most significant and effective Black literature will find a place in school and college curricula. I disagree with Professor J. Mitchell Morse, of Temple University, who stated in a recent article in *College English:*

> For many novels, stories, plays and poems that one would think could not be taken seriously by anybody who knows anything about the art are in fact taken seriously by many people—critics, re- viewers, teachers—who professionally profess to know quite a bit about it .... They are not

insensitive to literary values; often they have demonstrated a fine appreciation of nuances in works of the past; but in their belief that literature should speak to the problems of our time they tend to judge current fiction, drama and even poetry by other than literary standards. When they enter the present age they look for "relevance" above all: social relevance, political relevance, ethical relevance; and when they find it their enthusiasm often leads them to mistake it for literary relevance. . . .

They regard with approval and even with perverse pleasure all kinds of commonplace or sub-commonplace novels that attack racism or militarism or the TV industry or bigoted rural school boards. . . .[14]

In a report on a study of the crisis on college and university campuses the editors, who are college professors, point out that standard college courses in all fields have been severely criticized by students for their remoteness from the problems of the world that exists beyond the campus, and that society is already beginning to decay "when education ceases to be concerned with societal problems of the day." [15]

In the Preface of her *The New Novel in America,* Helen Wineberg says, "Reaction against the novel that had turned away from life toward aestheticism brought with it the rebirth of the novel that turned toward life. She concludes with the thought that the American novel in the sixties has renewed and extended inquiry into man's relations with his history, his society, and his politics, and "that it now seems possible to talk once again about a social environment and to take a stand in it and on it, whether the stand be an affirmation or an attack.[16] If Miss Wineberg's findings are valid, it appears that Professor Morse may have to give up reading contemporary literature because of its concern for what he calls extra-literary values, which he equates with aestheticism. Although he professes great concern about civil rights and the war in Vietnam, he seems to believe that novels concerning such subjects are always written by writers with "more heart than art." He says he will not tell his students that James Baldwin's *Another Country* is a good novel, and the tenor of his discussion indicates that he would not suggest to his students that they read it to see whether or not they can find any satisfying literary pleasures in it. He does not hesitate to assume this Olympian wisdom despite the fact that he knows (as all good teachers of literature should know) that "no amount of scholarly rigor or discretion can make any assertion in criticism more than a subjective speculation, yet it is often used to justify massive dogmatism and inflexibility."[17] As long as critics, scholars, and teachers with attitudes similar to those of Professor Morse prevail, significant Black literature will continue to be excluded from serious consideration in school and college classrooms.

NOTES

1. Emil Staiger, "The Questionable Nature of Value Problems." In *Problems of Literary Evaluation,* edited by Joseph Strelka (Philadelphia, Univ. of Penn. Press, 1969), p. 199.

2. John H. Fisher, "Movement in English," *ADE Bulletin* (September 1969): 41.

3. Robert F. Hogan, "The Future of the Profession," *ADE Bulletin* (September 1969): 46.

4. Alfred Kazin, "Form and Anti-form in Contemporary Literature," *The Barat Review* (June/July 1969).

5. Alfred Kazin, *On Native Grounds* (New York: Doubleday, 1956), p. 331.

6. Ibid., p. 334.

7. Ibid., p. 339.

8. Ibid., p. 341.

9. Larry Neal, *Black Theatre* 41 (Summer 1966): 30.

10. See Melvin Tolson, *Libretto for the Republic of Liberia* (New York: Twanye Publishers, 1953).

11. Robert A. Bone, *The Negro Novel in America* (New Haven, Yale U.P., 1958) p. 253.

12. Ibid., pp. 126-132.

13. Donald Hall, ed., *Contemporary American Poetry* (Baltimore: Penguin Books, 1967), p. 17.

14. J. Mitchell Morse, "The Case for Irrelevance," *College English* 30 (December 1968): 210-211.

15. Joseph Axelrod et al., *Search for Relevance* (San Francisco: Jossey-Bass,1969), p. 66.

16. Helen Wineberg, *The New Novel in America* (Ithaca: Cornell Univ. Press, 1970), p. ix-xvii.

17. Peter H. Elbow, "The Definition of Teaching," *College English* 30 (December 1969): 194.

GHETTOIZATION AND BLACK LITERATURE

John Bayliss

Walt Whitman, in his *Democratic Vistas*, wrote,

> Books are to be called for and supplied on the
> assumption that the process of reading is not
> half-sleep, but in the highest sense a gymnast's
> struggle; that the reader is to do something for
> himself, must be on the alert, must himself or
> herself construct indeed the poem, argument,
> history, metaphysical essay—the text furnishing the
> hints, the clue, the start or framework. Not the
> book needs so much to be the complete thing, but
> the reader of the book does. That we're to make a
> nation of supple and athletic minds, well trained,
> intuitive, used to depend on themselves and not on
> a few coteries of the writer.

John F. Bayliss

As we tackle the various issues of Black American literature studies, let us not forget our overall academic commitment, our context, so well summed up by Whitman. The university or school should be a family unit where intellectual intensity and honesty are paramount. With regard to Black literature study, I am beginning to question the quality of the gymnastics. At convention after convention one can hear whining non-Black professors and teachers asking for advice on how to teach Black literature. They advertise their empty heads. If the academic should be used to depending on himself, if he has developed a supple and athletic mind, then surely the combination of his reading and intelligence should have raised many key questions—and posited some answers. I make a plea for fearlessness in these studies. Black literature is not some ghetto, some Black cave, from which, if one knocks hard enough, someone will eventually emerge to offer a few goodies.

Nowhere is the lack of intellectual vigor so apparent as with the administrators of English departments. Let it be stated categorically that the White can no longer be hired to teach Black literature in an institution of higher learning in the United States. It is Blacks only for Black studies. But what is the reasoning? None. The White administrator sighs apologetically over the publications and good teaching credentials of the White applicant and then writes, "Unfortunately the pressure of the community and college is so great that we can hire only a Black." He then pays his twenty thousand dollar ransom money and receives his correctly colored professor. One notices a complete lack of intellectual fiber in the transaction; one hundred percent expediency operates. The administrator and his department can return to *Beowulf* emendations and Shakespeare cruxes, to working with noses deep in text and eyes oblivious to the centrality of the debate on ethnic literatures. Black literature is left in its ghetto of neglect. I make the plea that all department heads make it their duty to read some Black literature, ponder the issues involved and cease this countrywide cynicism with regard to hiring in Black studies.

By the ghettoization of Black literature, I mean the conscious or unconscious, the calculated or noncalculated blotting-out or separation of Black literature from the educational curriculum. In the past, a curricular ghetto was formed around this literature so that it was unobtainable both by the general student body and even by the predominantly Negro schools and colleges. (One hears of a priceless African collection being allowed to rot in the basement of a Negro college in the South. I myself lectured in 1967 at a long-established Black college in the South and propounded there, to an obviously uninitiated audience, that Black literature gave the race a helluva lot to be proud of. I was told that I was the best thing that hit that university in five years.) Since 1967, with the phenomenal rise of Black studies courses, a new ghetto has been forming around Black literature, a ghetto in which the Black community clutches its literature to itself as something understandable only to Blacks and which becomes contaminated if touched by any but Blacks. If my definition of ghettoization seems ambiguous, be assured, so is the reality.

71

First, let me dwell on the older, ongoing ghetto of neglect. It goes without saying that the following cynical cliché continues to bombard from every corner: "Have the Blacks a literature? If they have, it certainly is not worth studying." The past history of textbook publication, particularly, gives ample evidence of this cynicism, while the present publishing boom in Black studies shows a first denting of the attitude. Robert E. Morsberger of California State Polytechnic College, in a recent article *(Negro American Literature Forum*, Spring 1970), outlines the catastrophic neglect in the leading school and college anthologies:

> To my astonishment, I found that the third edition of *The Literature of the United States* (Scott, Foresman, 1966), a distinguished text edited by Walter Blair, Theodore Hornberger, Randall Stewart, and James E. Miller, Jr., has a total of 3097 pages in two volumes but does not include a single selection by a Negro except for three anonymous spirituals.

> The long respected and widely adopted *American Poetry and Prose*, ed. Norman Foerster (Houghton Mifflin, 1962), has 1638 pages of text, of which the only Afro-American selections are two anonymous spirituals, "Go Down Moses" and "Swing Low, Sweet Chariot." The fifth edition, due in the summer of 1969, will include only one piece by a Negro, an excerpt from *Invisible Man*.

> The four-volume *Viking Portable Library American Literature Survey*, ed. Milton R. Stern and Seymour L. Gross, has no Afro-American selections in its 2522 pages.

Anthologies of major authors, such as Holt, Rine-
hart and Winston's *American Literary Masters* (2
volumes, 2408 pages), include no Blacks at all.

Morsberger ends his article by showing the beginnings of a
change in the anthologies, but the English educator cannot
rest here with the vague feeling that things are righting
themselves. The April 6, 1970 issue of *Time* magazine,
devoted to Blacks in America, bludgeons out in a series of
situation reports the ghetto of neglect for the Black in
general. The picture is a sad one and the statistics show the
wasted years since Reconstruction. For example, with
housing,

> Black Americans pay more than whites for com-
> parable housing, and are four times more likely to
> live in substandard housing. In Black slums, hous-
> ing density (3,071 units per sq. mi.) is almost
> double that of middle-class urban areas, and 100
> times greater than in the suburbs . . . . Of all black
> Americans, including non-slum dwellers, says
> *Time*'s Harris poll, 25% have leaky ceilings, 26%
> are overcrowded, 29% say they have rats, 32%
> complain of faulty plumbing, and 38% report
> having cockroaches.

English educators, individually and especially collectively through their organizations, should dedicate themselves
to the task of giving the minorities a chance to be part of the
total America, on their own terms. No English education
class should feel at ease if it has not worked outside the
university with the inner city schools and poor children; no
English professor should feel at ease if Blake's *Songs of*

73

Experience does not have a modern equivalent and if he does not feel an obligation to add his mite to upgrading the minorities. The Modern Language Association and the National Council of Teachers of English should not feel at ease until they have instituted massive campaigns among their members to garner funds for minority-group scholarships (especially for the Indian); until they have forthrightly censured publishers for discrimination; until they have instituted checks on hiring practices throughout the profession; until they have lent their weight to the debate on integrated education; until they have helped fund minority culture centers; until they have diverted educators to work, at least part-time, in urban centers; until they have instituted massive research on the problems of English education and the ghetto child. How can we blandly give priority to convention lectures on the delights of poetry when ghetto children continue to have texts and tests and teachers not geared to them at all.

I am not here censuring the MLA and NCTE, but I am trying to infuse a sense of urgency which will dramatically change the priorities. (In passing, it should be noted that in 1969 the president of NCTE and the national convention chairman were both Blacks. This was no tokenism, but symbolic of an in-depth integration of the organization over the years.)

These preoccupations with the minorities, pondered with a sense of urgency, should not be tainted with paternalism, with "aiding the disadvantaged." Rather, the English educator and his organizations should see his efforts in the historical context of America, a country renowned for its dynamism. This is a solemn moment in history, as the remaining minorities butt their way into the total America, at the same time offering so much to America by their struggle. As Ralph Ellison pointed out in the April 2, 1970 *Time* essay:

> Materially, psychologically and culturally, part of the nation's heritage is Negro American, and whatever it becomes will be shaped in part by the Negro's presence. Which is fortunate, for today it is the black American who puts pressure on the nation to live up to its ideals. . . . But for blacks there are no hiding places down here, not in suburbia or in penthouses, neither in country nor in city. They are an American people who are geared to what *is* and who yet are driven by a sense of what is possible for human life to be in this society. The nation could not survive being deprived of their presence because by the irony implicit in the dynamics of American democracy, they symbolize both its most stringent testing and the possibility of its greatest human freedom.

Black American literature studies must be seen in the total context of America if a progressive atmosphere is to be engendered.

I now turn my attention to that other ghettoization of Black literature, the move to keep Black studies strictly for Blacks. The proliferation of Black studies courses and Black studies centers at the end of the 1960s will go down in educational history as one of the phenomena of the century. The continuance or the end of these movements is lost in the crystal ball of the future. Here, in California, one has only to look at the article by John Dreyfus (*Los Angeles Times*, April 25, 1969), "Ethnic Studies in State Mostly Promises, Plans," to see the enormous potential commitment to Black studies. And the sheer numbers of these courses throughout the country must impinge on the awareness of even the most traditional.

Have these studies already set themselves in the separatist mold? Have the study centers become separatist camps? DeVere E. Pentony in his perceptive article, "The Case for Black Studies" (*Atlantic*, April 1969), raises the problems of separatism but shows that by comparison with existing institutions there is little to fear and much to be gained in the individual thrust of Black studies:

> Will black studies scholars manipulate data, bias their studies, and create towering myths which bear little resemblance to the shifting realities of human existence? The answer is difficult to assess.
>
> In one respect the quest for pristine outside objectivity may miss the point. ... It may be that one of the most important roles that the black scholar can play is to share in the discovery and articulation of this normative inner order of the black community, with the possible result of improving the chances for mutually beneficial black-white interaction.

I myself fear the greatest danger for the Black studies movement, and for the Black Power movement, is that the Black student will be pushed into a psychological ghetto. Besides such positive thinking as "Black is Beautiful," the

Black student is having dinned into him that Western civilization is a white-livered, exploitative monstrosity, and that the Ethiopian is a pure and vastly superior culture. To me, this indoctrination is harmful and pernicious. It is all very well for the intellectual to say that hard Whitey deserves a hard Black response, but the actual outcome is racial strife. The Black is made to crawl back into history. Whereas his ancestors were able to sense "poor White trash" when they met up with it, the young Black of today must see all Whites and their civilization as trash, and this is catastrophic myth-making. Whereas his African brothers have with great perception and dignity culled what they felt was positive in Western culture, the young Black American is forced to look only within his Blackness, as something cut off from America, Africa, the East, and the West.

I would make a strong plea that the pundits of Black nationalism reassess their emphases, that they ease up on their superdefensive attitudes. Instead of the young Black luxuriating in the pride of his Blackness and in the joy of being able to partake in the fruits of other cultures, we come upon the dismal spectacle of Wesleyan University, where several races are crazy—instead of one. "The Two Nations at Wesleyan University" by Richard J. Margolis (*New York Times*, January 18, 1970) refers to this present madness.

> But cocoons come in several colors at Wesleyan, as they do elsewhere in America. The blacks have their Ujamaa; the whites have their centuries-old brotherhood of inherited wealth and power . . . and the school's handful of Puerto Rican students

have their newly formed Latin Leadership Conference, which specifically excludes Mexican-
Americans.

Black American literature studies must take cognizance
of this new ghettoizing, this separatist thrust among young
Blacks, and I feel, for the sake of integrity, for the sake of
truth, which can be arrived at only when all points of view
are aired, that teachers, scholars, and students must strive for
an internationalizing of Black studies courses. Otherwise, the
study of Black literature will become a study where only one
body of opinion may be heard; it will become a narrow
ghetto of reference. By internationalizing I mean, first, the
dispassionate study of Black literature by all. Second, I mean
the study of Black literatures other than American (especially
African and West Indian writing in English and French) and
this should include Black literature by non-Blacks such as
Sartre and Genet. Third, Black American literature should be
studied against the totality of man's written creation.

Benjamin F. Payton, President of Benedict College, ably
summed up this international aesthetic in the March 1969
issue of *Negro Digest*.

A functional Black University will strive to engage
in the kind of teaching and research and public
service which provides people with the disciplines
of thought and action by which they can mature as
persons and help shape the world into a more
human place of habitation. The irremediable blackness of Afro-Americans would be accepted both as
a fact of life and as a positive value. But, it would
not restrict the experience of black identity to the

immediacies of skin-associated cultural values. The black experience is one crucible in which we work our way to a vision of and a connection with the human potential of all men.

Within this international context, this de-ghettoizing of Black literature, one must finally come upon the vexing question of who should teach this literature and who should be a critic of it. Have we already acquired a ghetto of Black teachers and critics, a national coterie, at which all other critics must peer in awe? I am firmly convinced that there is a fallacy in the argument which legislates that Blacks only may teach and criticize Black literature. The fallacy is that living Black and writing Black must be taken as synonymous. They are not. The writing down of experience internationalizes that experience; the part of a culture that can be transmitted is filtered through literature to the whole world community. Miss Carolyn Gerald (*Negro Digest*, January 1970) befuddles this issue by calling the English language a White tool. It is a neutral tool. If there are oysters in the language to be opened, such as in-words, difficult connotative core words, then the scholar (the Black scholar) can explicate them for all readers and end the momentary confusion. Miss Gerald writes:

> The artist, then, is the guardian of image; the writer is the myth-maker of his people. We still at times are not sure as to how much of our image is us; to what extent we are the sole authors of our myth, our peoplehood. There are those white people who would nullify any argument we advance on the basis that it is advanced in a white

language. And it is true that languages project a specific cultural image. But I believe that we have arrived at a stage of self-awareness in our writing which sees this type of argument as irrelevant.

Professor Joseph Keller, in the Winter 1969 issue of *Negro American Literature Forum*, tries to show how core words must permanently befuddle the White critic. I would postulate that he is confusing the living experience itself with that transmitted by literature. Even the Black teacher of Black literature can use only language to define what is already transmitted from experience into language. I shall briefly note some points in the interesting Keller thesis to show the complexity of the core word motifs—but also to hint that they are not unsurmountable.

> Obviously, the motifs of black writing are many. They are motifs of oppression and/or of identification. . .
>
> —motifs of physical identification ("Winds of Change" by Loyle Hairston: kinds of hair style; skin color: "Reena" by Paule Marshall)
>
> —motifs of verbal identification (speech patterns, Biblical phrases, folklore, proverb, sermon as in Ben Caldwell's *Prayer Meeting*).

It is noteworthy how in the succinct but helpful article that ends the *Time* magazine special on the Black American, that the fundamental problem of semantics within the literature is again tackled. In the extract from this section, on Black poetry specifically, I would ask the reader to bear in mind the possibilities of what can be explicated from an international context of reference, rather than from a teacher explaining from a Black experience.

> For a white man to read LeRoi Jones or almost any other black poet is like being held in a dark room while listening to an angry voice threaten him in a language he is not expected to appreciate or understand. . . .

> "Black English" is not an illiterate language, as many think, but remarkably rich in nuances. According to Toni Morrison, an editor at Random House, "many of these poets are turning to the grammar, the punctuation, the language through which subculture blacks in particular have resisted total Westernization. Black dialect—if you want to call it that—is probably more subtle and sophisticated than standard White English." In standard English, she says, "There are only two present tenses—I work, I am working. In English, as spoken in White Appalachia, there are three—I work, I am working, I a' working. In Black Appalachian dialect, there are five. . . .

Besides the possible misdirection of the semantic debate concerning the understanding and criticism of Black literature, there is some outright special pleading being perpetrated. Hoyt Fuller, in his excellent but provocative editorials in *Negro Digest* would have us believe that the White critic is always listened to more than the Black. He feels that Robert Bone is an evil influence because everybody swears by him, when in reality Black scholars such as Brawley, Redding, Gloster, and Locke have been, and continue to be, regarded as the authorities. Fuller asserts:

But the White Literary Establishment is not willing to release its stranglehold on black literature. It has been traditional, of course, that white critics decided what was valuable and valid in black literature. Robert A. Bone, for one, has been floating along for years on a reputation as the leading "authority" on black literature on the basis of his book, *The Negro Novel in America.* In most academic circles, Mr. Bone cannot be challenged by a black writer or critic; his judgement is final, his taste infallible.

I would suggest that this raising of the shibboleth of "White experts" is bunkum. Scholarship does not work at that level of naiveté. For example, Bone has been carefully analyzed by the Black critic, and the criticisms have been assumed into the total record. But the praise Bone has received has not been invalidated; he can give the Black scholar a good run for his money.

If the White critic can criticize Black literature, so also can he teach it. As Dr. Martin Kitson, a Black assistant professor at Harvard put it,

> Of course, it is possible for a white to teach these courses. If he can't, he can't teach anything else. If whites can't teach about Black culture, we should all stop studying foreign cultures of any kind— Chinese, Irish, whatever. The American Black is not a Yoruba, but he assumes he can study Yoruba even though it is a culture to him. (*New York Times*, April 6, 1970).

In conclusion, I will refer to a recent article, "The Reincarnation of John Monro" (*New York Times*, March 15,

1970), which reminds us of the special qualities needed to enter the inner sanctum (not ghetto) of Black studies. For years, Whites, as well as Blacks, have deeply understood and appreciated that "Black is beautiful," and that the study of Blackness is a delicate and demanding art. John Monro gave up the deanship of Harvard College to devote his energies to teaching Black students at Miles College in Alabama. The following extracts should spell out a lesson to us all:

> The question of a white teacher's role in a Black college has become more pressing at Miles recently, especially in the light of what Monro calls "a measurably more militant atmosphere last fall."

> "There's much greater attention paid now to Black awareness than there used to be," Monro says. "But this is proper. This is what this college ought to be about. Any Black college worth a damn has got to be militant about the Black community. I don't regard this as a threat, but some white teachers here have expressed serious doubts about their role."

> Says President Pitts: "Whites who come to a Black college need to come as John has come—naked. Naked in the sense that he's come not just to give but to receive, as a participating learner and contributor. If he does that, then the sky's the limit. John's willingness to give of himself, to do his share of committee work without complaining, settled in the minds of the faculty that he wasn't coming here to throw his weight around but was ready to join the community. Here he cast his lot."

THE CHALLENGE OF BLACK
LITERATURE: NOTES ON INTERPRETATION

James A. Emanuel

John Milton, in his famous *Areopagitica*, reasoned that "as good almost kill a man as kill a good book." The 1970s, fringing our shameful years of assassination and deterioration of public morality, might amply testify to the truth of Milton's next observation: "Many a man lives a burden to the earth; but a good book is the precious life-blood of a master spirit, embalmed and treasured up on purpose to a life beyond life." The current attention commanded by Black literature is fixed upon an unspoken question: In the hard-faced spilling of life-blood that defines the career of the Black race in America, how many master spirits have been

turned away from the door of the academy? The question
will be asked and answered, but the labor of responding will
be secondary to what has always been the daily task and
challenge of the individual student of literature: intimate,
honest engagement with representative works. American men
of letters are immediately challenged to make their profession democratically meaningful by discovering and treasur-
ing the contributions of Black authors. It is the purpose of
the following observations to stimulate the exercise of critical
faculties by those attracted to what James Weldon Johnson
felt to be "the power and beauty of the minstrel's lyre" in
the long line of Black and unknown bards.

Among these relatively unknown bards—and the word
bards is extended in these remarks to include Black authors
of prose as well as poetry—Jean Toomer is one of the earliest
whose work promises to brave ready analysis until formidable
critics set themselves to the task of achieving some consensus
regarding his one major work, a combination of stories,
poems, sketches, and a uniquely structured play, entitled
Cane (1923). Taking up the challenge of interpreting *Cane*,
Robert Bone calls the book "frustrating,"[1] Arna Bontemps
labels it "hard to classify,"[2] Edward Margolies decides that it
is "very nearly impossible to describe,"[3] and Todd Lieber
finds it "exasperating."[4] One of the earliest commentators,
Hugh M. Gloster, and one of the most recent, Darwin T.
Turner, record their observations without measuring the
difficulty. The detailed remarks of Turner and Lieber set
forth in essays published in 1969 in *Negro Digest* and *CLA
Journal*, respectively, evidence the increasing intensity with

which Toomer and, by implication, other Black writers are being examined. It should serve the cause of a full exploration of this neglected literary tradition, then, to suggest a few interpretations that might be considered and a few inquiries that might be made regarding several works by Toomer and his fellow writers. The sense of crisis that pervades all serious deliberations upon this subject might be eased by the fact that many varieties of taste can be fully satisfied by this literary adventure, ranging from aesthetic appreciation of symbols and images to utilitarian approval of the Black consciousness and positive racial reflections being urged today upon writers in this tradition.

Just as Langston Hughes's well known "The Negro Speaks of Rivers" expresses an eighteen-year-old poet's love for his race, Jean Toomer's "Song of the Son" reveals self-dedication to the same ancestral past. The verbal subtleties of Toomer's poem, a work which is autobiographically as fascinating as Hughes's, commend themselves to faculties conditioned to savor the individual word. Those subtleties are obvious in the following lines, in which Toomer speaks directly to his ancestral land and soil:

> Now just before an epoch's sun declines
> Thy son, in time, I have returned to thee,
> Thy son, I have in time returned to thee.
>
> In time, for though the sun is setting on
> A song-lit race of slaves, it has not set.

Then, speaking to his forbears, the poet closes with two stanzas that meld beauty and truth with a perhaps unapparent artistry:

O Negro slaves, dark purple ripened plums,
Squeezed, and bursting in the pine-wood air,
Passing, before they stripped the old tree bare
One plum was saved for me, one seed becomes

An everlasting song, a singing tree,
Caroling softly souls of slavery,
What they were, and what they are to me,
Caroling softly souls of slavery (p. 21).

Phrases and ideas in this poem connect with Langston Hughes's "Jazzonia," first published the same year as *Cane*; connect with Yeats's "A Prayer for My Daughter," published two years earlier; and connect with Whitman's "Crossing Brooklyn Ferry." With no thought of comparison, Toomer's poem can be analyzed by recourse to its images of light, of sound, and of vegetation. His skill with images is glimpsed in the fact that he uses plums in at least six different ways, all adding to the historical and bardic meanings of the poem.

Toomer's stories, sketches, and imaginatively structured play entitled "Kabnis," although they have been perceptively commented upon in some detail by Professors Bone, Turner, and Lieber, require intensive study and explication. The story, "Box Seat," which vividly protests man's subordination to a machine-ridden, hypocritically moral society, has an expressionistic style that immediately commends the genius of the author as one meriting comparison to Eugene O'Neill, who had, the year before, revealed his own genius in the publication and production of *The Hairy Ape*. Instructive comparisons might be drawn between characters in these two pioneer expressionistic works: between Toomer's Dan and

O'Neill's Yank, between Toomer's Muriel and O'Neill's Mildred, and between Toomer's bloody dwarf in the boxing ring who crushes the pretension of Muriel and O'Neill's hairy ape that crushes the life out of Yank.

Similarly informative would be a comparison of the role of Toomer's Mrs. Pribby and Albert Camus' robot-woman in *The Stranger.* "There is a sharp click," writes Toomer, as Mrs. Pribby "fits into her chair and draws it to the table. The click is metallic like the sound of a bolt being shot into place" (p. 107). Camus writes that his nameless mechanical woman, taking a seat beside Meursault in Céleste's restaurant, "moved in a curiously jerky way, as if she were on wires."[5] She wears a close-fitting jacket, pays the exact sum of her bill in advance, takes out a blue pencil to tick off the daily programs on her radio magazine, then walks out with "abrupt, robotlike gestures." "The rows of houses" in Washington, D.C., Toomer writes, "belong to other Mrs. Pribbys" (p. 107). Describing Muriel's chair as "close and stiff about her," the author expressionistically boxes her in further with "the rows of houses locked about her chair" (p. 113). When Dan tries to sing to these houses, his voice cracks and the effort hurts his throat. In Camus' story, when Meursault tries to explain to the court the cruel physiological effect upon him of the hot sun at the moment of the crime, his words become jumbled and the audience snickers. Both protagonists, one facing an awakening to life and the other an awakening to death, fail to communicate with a mechanical society mired in hypocritical, deadening routines. "Row-houses and row-lives," then — to borrow a line from

James A. Emanuel

Baltimorean Karl Shapiro's poem "The Dome of Sunday"—are the important theme of Toomer's story.

One-third of *Cane*—over eighty pages in the Perennial Classic reprint of 1969—is taken up by "Kabnis," which is divided into six scenes in rural Georgia. Robert Bone, beginning the present resurgent interest in *Cane* in his study *The Negro Novel in America* (1958), briefly characterizes the cast in "Kabnis" and mentions the dramatic movement of the action. Darwin Turner, also focusing upon characterization, introduces some doubt regarding the clarity of thematic unity in "Kabnis" and concludes that Toomer ends "with obvious pessimism."[6] Todd Lieber finds thematic unity in the fact that all the characters are shown reacting to Father John, the symbolic, ancient Black man who lives silently in Halsey the handyman's cellar, itself reminiscent of a slave ship. Lieber argues that *Cane* thematically moves from the beauty and value of Black Southern heritage in Part I, through Northern stagnation and distortion of that heritage in Part II, to its creative recovery in Part III in "Kabnis"—a communion approximating that established by Toomer himself on his journey to the South with Waldo Frank the year before *Cane* was published. Preserving his thesis, Lieber finds much more optimism at the end of the book than Turner does, although both critics reach their conclusions through the same method, through reference to some character other than Kabnis. Turner sees a mere "ray of optimism" in the figure of Lewis, an educated Black man from the North who secures a degree of rapport with people of his race in the South. Lieber, by shifting his attention to young Carrie Kate,

90

Halsey's sister, determines that "Toomer's goal [in *Cane*] has been achieved" because the girl does lovingly accept the blind and deaf old man, not only in his reflection of "his intrinsic beauty and vitality," but also in his representation of pain and anguish in their common racial past.

Published analyses of *Cane*, exemplified by these selections from observations on "Kabnis," cannot yet be expected to have dealt adequately with all categories of substance in the book, not to mention all its specific important details. Some of the unexplored, challenging pathways into the center of *Cane* might be sufficiently indicated by further reference to "Kabnis." That semiautobiographical work by a "prose lyricist," as Turner calls the author, understandably pursues the significant theme of the artist versus society. Kabnis is surely to be considered an artist. He so designates himself, complaining when Halsey shakes him in his cellar bunk that "it's preposterous t root an artist out o bed at this ungodly hour" (p. 227), that is, after a night of debauchery with the girls. At the very start of the play, Kabnis muses over his own duality as follows:

> Ralph Kabnis is a dream. And dreams are faces with large eyes and weak chins and broad brows that get smashed by the fists of square faces. The body of the world is bull-necked. A dream is a soft face that fits uncertainly upon it . . . [*sic*] God, if I could develop that in words. Give what I know a bull-neck and a heaving body, all would go well with me. . . (p. 158).

Before the reader reaches the crucial dialogue pertaining to this theme at the end of Scene 5, he sees Kabnis' dilemma as a writer illuminated against another art and against a different artistic personality. Halsey the handyman, passing a bottle of "corn licker" to Kabnis, says that "th boys what made this stuff have got th art down like I heard you say youd like t be with words" (p. 184). Halsey, himself, is given the role of an artist. "An artist in your way, arent you, Halsey?" Lewis suggests. Halsey replies affirmatively and adds that "there aint no books whats got th feel t them of them there tools" (pp. 200-201). But the broadly racial meaning of this reply is revealed only later in Scene 5, where Halsey tells Lewis about important events in his cultural background: his inability to secure an education in post-Reconstruction Georgia without surrendering both pride and privacy, despite the advantage of his light complexion, and his unsuccessful attempt to nurture his mind afterwards through subscriptions to the *Literary Digest*, which did not provide him with anything that, in his own words, he could sink his teeth into. Halsey represents the perversion of love and the diminution of cultural inclination caused by racism: Stella, whom he once loved, he can now call a "common wench" (p. 220); he spends his life "shapin shafts and buildin wagons" (p. 188). In artistic terms, although Halsey "lifts an oak-beam, fingers it, and becomes abstracted" (p. 228), his materials generally control his purposes, leaving him free only to mend, never to change or to interpret material objects in his life.

Shaping wood and metal in his workshop to fit customers' demands, Halsey thinks that similar activity will "make a man of" Kabnis, but Kabnis cannot even mend a broken hatchet brought in by an old White man. The reason for his failure is important to the theme of the artist versus society. Working with tense concentration on the hatchet, Kabnis "feels stifled. Through Ramsay [the old White man], the whole White South weighs down upon him" (p. 201). Halsey takes the hatchet and fixes it "with a few deft strokes" (p. 202). The handyman's superior skill is compared with true creative artistry in Scene 5, when the three men and two women descend into "the Hole," the name given to the cellar, for a night of dissipation. There, Kabnis shakes his finger in Halsey's face and tells him:

> . . .youre all right f choppin things from blocks of wood. I was good at that th day I ducked th cradle. An since then, I've been shapin words after a design thats branded here. Know whats here? M soul. . . . Been shapin words t fit m soul.

Kabnis continues vigorously to explain his dilemma:

> Those words . . . wont fit int th mold thats branded on m soul. Rhyme, y see? Poet, too. Bad rhyme. Bad poet. . . . Th form thats burned int my soul is some twisted awful thing that crept in from a dream, a godam nightmare, an wont stay still unless I feed it. An it lives on words. . . . Misshapen, split-gut, tortured, twisted words (pp. 223-24).

Kabnis laments bitterly that such words are fed into his soul by evil people, both Black and White. He says, "This whole damn bloated purple country feeds it cause its goin down t hell in a holy avalanche of words. I want t feed th soul—I know what that is; th preachers dont—but *I've* [italics are mine] got t feed it" (p. 224).

Kabnis, then, in almost two pages of half-drunken speech, is disclosing that his soul once rhymed and that beautiful words fit his inner life, but that now it is perversely accustomed to being fed evil words by an evil society. Kabnis has lost his control over his own spiritual nurture in an environment that has lost its love. His dilemma as an artist complicates his predicament as a Black man, for as an artist he insists that "no eyes that have seen beauty ever lose their sight" (p. 232). Father John, being blind, could have seen no beauty; hence, there was no beauty in Kabnis' ancestral past, and he cannot identify himself with it any more than he can accept the evil now encompassing him.

Yet, the artist in Kabnis increases the possibility of his acceptance of his racial past as embodied in the old man, for when Father John repetitiously murmurs the word *death*, Kabnis "forgets the old man as his mind begins to play with the word and its associations" (p. 231). Then he realizes that both he and the old man are in the environs of slavery, now twenty feet under ground, "where they used t throw th worked-out, no-count slaves. On a damp clammy floor of a dark scum-hole. An they called that an infirmary" (p. 233). And he must concede usable knowledge in Father John as he says "T hell with you," for he must immediately add, "You know what hell is cause youve been there" (p. 232). Although Kabnis can later scorn the old man's outdated muttering about White people's sins, as an artist he has felt the meaning of Father John's bodily existence. Once the

former slave murmurs the single word *sin*, Kabnis applies it to
the plight of the Black man as artist, precluding any further
significance that the patriarch could add. Kabnis senses with
vexation that the old man is his responsibility as an artist—as
Toomer's thematic poem "Song of the Son" predicts—the
vexation proceeding from his own knowledge of how
America, especially the South, has brutally complicated his
task. Sounding like a combination of Hawthorne and
Thoreau, modified by a Black man's understanding, Kabnis
tells the old man to shut up and explains to Carrie Kate:

> It was only a preacher's sin they knew in those old
> days, an that wasnt sin at all. Mind me, th only sin
> is whats done against th soul. Th whole world is a
> conspiracy t sin, especially in America, an against
> me. I'm th victim of their sin. I'm what sin is (p.
> 236).

This emphasis upon a portion of the poetry and prose in
Cane has been a deference to chronology in the tradition of
already acclaimed, imaginative Black literature as much as it
has been a suggestion of the relative thrust of the challenge of
a more thorough interpretation. If one were to explore the
problems of the artist as they have been revealed in Black
literature, he would turn to, among other works in the several
genres, the novel, *Blood on the Forge* (1941), by William
Attaway; to the short story, "The Blues I'm Playing" (1934),
by Langston Hughes; and to the poem, "The Egg Boiler"
(1960), by Gwendolyn Brooks. The role of religion in Black
America, another theme found in "Kabnis," is reflected in
the novel, *Black Thunder* (1936), by Arna Bontemps; in the

short story, "Fire and Cloud" (1938), by Richard Wright; in the poem, "Heritage" (1925), by Countee Cullen; and in other works in each literary form. Love and power in relationships between Black men and Black women (seen in Toomer's "Carma" more clearly than in "Kabnis") can be traced in a number of works, including the novel, *Ollie Miss* (1935), by George Wylie Henderson; the short story, "So Peaceful in the Country" (1945), by Carl Offord; and the poem, "I Am a Black Woman" (1969), by Mari Evans.

The task—perhaps *privilege* would be a more appropriate word—of identifying and interpreting the most important novels, short stories, poems, plays, and essays in Black literature must be accepted by increasing numbers of serious critics. New and corrective analyses of major novels like *Native Son* and *Invisible Man* are imperative now, lest misconceptions and oversights be confirmed through neglect. *Native Son*, for example, should be examined as a work of literary art—a viewpoint implicit in my essay on its imagery published in the issue of *Negro Digest* especially devoted to Richard Wright (December 1968). The standard criticism that the end of *Native Son* bogs down in Communist propaganda needs to be reconsidered. As for *Invisible Man*, its richness in both literary art and racial substance is so varied that several small volumes of commentary, each taking a different approach, could be written about that novel by any sensitive scholar who has read it closely. The list of Black novelists who have written creditably since World War II and who remain ignored by critics of the Establishment is sufficiently long to induce some despair over the probability of balanced literary judgment in the university community. Chester Himes, Ann Petry, and Dorothy West, who started writing novels in the 1940s, should be known, especially the first two. From the 1950s, one must salvage, besides Baldwin, among those who in that decade began their careers as novelists, William Demby, Julian Mayfield, Paule Marshall, and John O. Killens. In the 1960s, there appeared novelists who merit serious attention, among them Gordon Parks, Ronald Fair, John A. Williams, LeRoi Jones, Charles Wright, William Melvin Kelley, and Ernest J. Gaines. Reaching back to the 1930s, one must not overlook Zora Neale Hurston.

The brevity of the short story and the poem as literary forms suggests that pertinent authors and titles are too numerous to list meaningfully in these closing remarks. It might suffice to mention a few examples of the many stimulating stories and poems that will abundantly reward close study. Langston Hughes's many sketches and several stories about Jesse B. Semple, who has been ranked with Huckleberry Finn as a major character in American literature, contain about twenty separate styles of humor, still unanalyzed by critics. About a dozen of the sixty-six short stories published by Hughes deserve full critical examination, among them "Father and Son," "Big Meeting," and "On the Road." Ralph Ellison's prize-winning story, "Flying Home," is a masterful illumination, in both the philosophical and the pictorial sense, of the phrase "Black is beautiful." Ellison's story "King of the Bingo Game" pictures a Black man whose economic plight and love for his wife drive him to the brink of hysteria and on to visionary access to racial truth. The author's symbolic use of an electrical extension cord in this story forecasts similar artistry in *Invisible Man*. Ernest J. Gaines, one of the best of the latest writers, is the author of "The Sky Is Gray," an unforgettable account of the pride and independence of a small Black boy and his mother as they endure freezing cold and hunger on their long trip to a dentist.

As for poetry, the general excellence of the few works about to be mentioned should not be minimized by the fact that in each case only one suggestion is given for gaining new insight into the art or content. It cannot be over-emphasized that a multitude of poems are exemplified by these few. DuBois' nineteenth-century poem, "The Song of the Smoke," contains in its sixth and seventh stanzas the reversal of stereotyped connotations of Blackness now being urged in the new Black aesthetics controversy. Claude McKay, in his sonnet, "The White House," using the "homicidal art" categorized in my essay in the book *Black Expression* (1969), compresses the tension, physiological torment, and determined humanity of Black people facing specific instances of prejudice. Countee Cullen's poem, "Magnets," which rhythmically expresses a brotherly philosophy focused on the word *need*, places that word in the exact center of the poem, in the middle of the middle line, where it becomes the fulcrum on which both meaning and structure turn. Langston Hughes's sensational poem, "Christ in Alabama," which almost started a riot in 1931 at the University of North Carolina, has an acrostic structure which places it among his experiments with topographical and emblematic verse. If

"Christ in Alabama" is read vertically, starting with either the first or the last word of the opening line, the result is a tight little poem for the 1970s. Gwendolyn Brooks' sonnet beginning "First fight. Then fiddle," exploring the phenomenon of violence, as viewed by an artist, uses allusions to the rituals of nineteenth-century thuggee in India. LeRoi Jones, in his mimeographed collection, *Black Art* (1966), includes among his verbally strange poems one entitled "A Chant to rise with all"; it jumbles the alphabet and mixes in numbers and words out of order, but inserts marvelously sane and clear phrases that speak directly of the spiritual dilemma of our times. That spiritual dilemma is the subject of much Black poetry being written at this moment by such popular authors as Don L. Lee. Lee's poem, "Assassination," vividly and sarcastically pictures one of the causes of that dilemma, whereas his poem, "A Message All Blackpeople Can Dig," foretells the desirable achievement of Lee and his "revolutionary" brother writers. His poem ends thus:

> blackpeople
> are moving, moving to return
>   this earth into the hands of
> human beings.[7]

The challenge to the academy on which it dares not turn its back is an invitation to move, intellectually at least, into the full honesty and freedom that long ago befitted all the human beings who came to these shores.

James A. Emanuel

NOTES

1. Robert Bone, *The Negro Novel in America*, rev. ed. (New Haven, Yale U.P. 1965), p. 88.

2. Arna Bontemps, "Introduction" to Perennial Classic reprint of *Cane* (New York, Harper, 1969), p. xii. All references to *Cane* will appear in the text.

3. Edward Margolies, *Native Sons: A Critical Study of Twentieth-Century Negro American Authors* (Philadelphia, Lippincott, 1968), p. 39.

4. Todd Lieber, "Design and Movement in *Cane*," *CLA Journal* 13, no. 1 (September 1969); 35.

5. Leo Hamalian and Edmond L. Volpe, eds., *Ten Modern Short Novels* (New York, Putnam, 1958), p. 591.

6. Darwin Turner, "Jean Toomer's *Cane*," *Negro Digest* 18, no. 3 (January 1969); 59.

7. Don L. Lee, *Don't Cry, SCREAM* (Detroit, Broadside, 1969), p. 64.

THE LETTERS OF RICHARD WRIGHT

Edward Margolies

It is scarcely necessary to justify the letters of any major writer, but in Richard Wright's case a few prefatory words need be said, for his letters carry something more than biographical value. In his lifetime he experienced the enormous historical changes wrought on the life of the Black man over the past fifty years. Passing as he did from the rural, communal, caste-ridden South to the depersonalized, anarchic bustle of the cities in the industrial North and thence to a kind of statelessness in Paris championing the rights of all the world's colored people, Wright seems almost to symbolize the changes he underwent. From one point of view, Wright

101

was not really very different from other Black people who chose exile, but almost from the very start of his authorial career, he was conscious of the changes his new conditions wrought on his outlook and he recorded these. He regarded himself as a writer writing in history, and nowhere is this consciousness more apparent than in his correspondence.

This is not to say that Wright's letters were all of one sort, but throughout many of them one sees Wright aiming for an historical perspective. His writings are important, if for no other reason, in that they record a sensitivity to how these changes have revolutionized the consciousness of a Black man several times over in a single lifetime—a process which for White America, as Wright frequently pointed out, took several centuries. His correspondents, whoever they may be, are thus often made recipients of Wright's racial, social, and world views regardless of what the original intent of the letters may have been. But Wright in this respect is seldom boring or intrusive; indeed, one feels from time to time that by writing out his ideas he is trying to understand them himself. There are, however, occasions when he is unintentionally funny: In his Communist Party period he writes an old Mississippi school chum, "How's your class consciousness coming along?"[1] That he may also sound pedantic is undeniable, but he is frequently insightful about the meaning of world affairs, and often his views are borne out by events. Indeed, he occasionally suggests (and here he is not very consistent) that his nonfiction travel books dealing with political, social, racial, and religious issues have more to say than his fiction. Fiction, he implies, may be a means of disguising disagreeable truths. He writes a correspondent in 1956 that he will do novels again because unadulterated "facts hurt people. They like their facts floated on the syrup of imagination."[2]

Before going more specifically into the contents of these letters, I will make a few general remarks about his correspondents. Well over half of the eight hundred or so letters collected thus far were written to Paul Reynolds, his friend, his literary advisor, and his literary agent; another considerable number he sent to Edward Aswell, an editor whom he first met at Harpers; he wrote another large batch to Margrit de Sabloniere, his Dutch translator, an ardent admirer of his works, and herself the author of a book on South Africa and apartheid. There were also several important letters to Gertrude Stein and a scattering of correspondence to personal friends, readers, friendly and hostile critics, and persons who might have been able to help Wright or Wright's friends in projects they wanted to undertake. For example, he wrote to Mrs. Roosevelt in 1938 to request her aid in recommending him for a Guggenheim fellowship; he wrote to his draft board in 1942 requesting a special officer's commission; he wrote to John Strachey, the Labor parliamentarian, in 1959 requesting his help in acquiring a visa to live permanently in England; he wrote to Alexander Korda in November 1950 suggesting he produce a film about Haiti and allow Wright to do the screenplay; he wrote to the Baroness Rothschild in 1948 for financial support for the periodical *Présence Africaine*; he wrote to Governor Thomas Edison of New Jersey in 1941 for clemency for the convict, Clinton

Brewer; he wrote to Mercer Cook and Edmund Wilson in the late 1950s requesting their aid in seeking financial support for a book he wished to do on French West Africa. In addition, there are letters to Alfred Knopf, Paul Reynolds, Edward Aswell, the Guggenheim judges, even Prime Minister Nehru of India, on behalf of such writers as Gwendolyn Brooks, Lawrence Lipton, Nelson Algren, Peter Abrahams, Bill Rutherford, Saunders Redding, and many more.

There are of course a number of important letters Wright sent off at one time or another that remain unobtainable. Among these are letters to Ralph Ellison, Margaret Walker, Horace Cayton, and maybe one or two each to Alain Locke, Countee Cullen and Melvin Tolson.

We have no letters to his family. He rarely wrote to his mother, brother, and aunt but made sure via Reynolds that they received financial assistance. Although for the last year of his life he lived apart from his wife and daughters who for the most part were staying in London, they kept in touch almost daily by telephone.[3] The greatest losses, however, are letters he wrote to George Padmore (an aide and advisor to Nkrumah who from the early 1930s had deeply involved himself in African nationalist movements) because these would have given us the best perspective on Wright's political growth in regard to Africa and the third world.

A word about the style of these letters: There is considerable variation in the care Wright took about his correspondence. If he felt or thought or hoped that his letter would be published—such as one reflecting his literary, political, or social viewpoints—the writing is precise, flowing, and toughly argued. There are a fair number of letters of this sort in the collection, several of which incidentally, have been published in periodicals and newspapers. However, the vast majority of his letters were not written for publication, and the writing in these—the phrasing, the syntax—occasionally leaves something to be desired. Wright was a prolific letter writer; he would often read and work on his manuscripts in the mornings and devote his afternoons to letters: business letters, letters to admirers, letters to persons who sought his advice or opinion, letters to editors of various publications, and finally, of course, letters to close friends like Joe Brown and the aforementioned Margrit de Sabloniere. But Wright was no Mme. de Sévigné; he did not regard letter writing as a literary genre; he wrote letters because he had to—not because he really wanted to. He was a man who liked to think of himself as always living in the present, and letters for him were an expression of the present. "Time does not mean much to me," he wrote in his journal (1945).

> I never bother about the past or other peoples'. And I dislike thinking about the future. I'm sunk into a *Now*, a living, breathing moment; each flow of time is an eternity to me. It is native with me, constitutional. That is why my work, my writing is so intense, an intensity that people mistake for bitterness.

His letters are a succession of nows, of coexistent but different nows to different correspondents. In a kind of broken line they retrace the trajectory of his life and career.

105

Once again, I return to the contents of these letters. First of all, they are invaluable to the biographer. Not only do they reveal where Wright was and when, and what he was doing, but they also take us behind the scenes of some rather significant moments in his life. We are witness to his anguish, frustration, and fury as he works under police state conditions in the shooting of his film *Native Son* in Argentina. We see him attempting to extricate himself tactfully from some rather involved business relationships with European publishers and agents. We observe him attempting to settle amicably a dispute that arose among the editors of *Présence Africaine*. We listen to his side of the story regarding journalists, publishers, and authors who he feels have misrepresented or betrayed him. In an open letter to Anna Louise Strong that was published in the Paris edition of the *Herald Tribune* in 1949, he angrily recalls some of the tensions and the controversies in the American Communist Party in the 1930s. Toward the end of his life, we find him almost desperately seeking some kind of writing assignment that would enable him to sustain pride in himself.

The letters, too, are a mine of information on Wright as a literary man. We learn that he often writes Reynolds or Aswell about how, when, or where he works and what he proposes to do next. Frequently we find him working on several projects simultaneously. We learn as well that the drafts of many of his celebrated works are almost twice as long as the published versions and that as a rule he almost always accepts the advice of editors or Reynolds regarding cuts, condensations, and even minor plot changes. He was apparently an ideal author for editors to work with, always cooperative, perhaps because he often felt unsure of the value of a book after he had written it.

We learn of many works of fiction—novels and stories (*Maud, Little Sister, Nine Men, The Jackal, Rite of Passage, Island of Hallucination*)—which for one reason or another have never been published. In regard to his travel books, *Black Power, Pagan Spain,* and *The Color Curtain,* we discover that he anticipated many of the underlying arguments or theses of these books before he even visited the countries.

Equally important, we learn the sources of some of Wright's published works. "The Man Who Lived Underground" for example is not so much influenced by Dostoyevsky as by a news story he read. Similarly, "The Man Who Killed A Shadow" and *Savage Holiday* derive from journalistic sources. On the other hand, we learn that much of *The Long Dream* was autobiography he never put into *Black Boy.*

There is one especially intriguing letter he wrote to Aswell in 1955 in which he outlines a series of novels he wants to do, each of which would be connected by a single theme: man's life, spirit, impulses, instincts in opposition to the necessarily repressive nature of organized society. Finally, we learn that for him writing was a matter of being alive, of feeling alive, that when he could not write, he literally suffered. In a 1960 letter to Margrit de Sabloniere, he says that without a manuscript to work on he feels spiritually depleted; writing for him, he continues, must be like psychoanalysis for others—it is a way of draining the poison from his system.

107

Curiously, the letters do not cast very much light on other writers who may have influenced him, although Wright was a very bookish man. He does make several favorable allusions to Faulkner in letters as far back as 1938. "Tell him for me," he wrote Joe Brown who was living in Oxford, Mississippi in the mid 1940s, "that he's a word-slinger from 'way back." Wright did carry on an occasional correspondence with some writers like Philip Wylie and Langston Hughes. He later became friends with some of his literary correspondents—for example, Paul Green, Carl Van Vechten, and Dorothy Norman. One of the authors he had always admired was Gertrude Stein, and when she wrote from Paris in 1945 how much she liked *Black Boy*, Wright was delighted. There ensued an exchange of letters between them for about a year, after which time Wright went to Paris where he met her. Contrary to his usual letter-writing procedure, he would write several drafts of a letter to her before he mailed it, which in itself suggests how deferential he must have felt. Within a short span of time, however, he becomes less inhibited and relates at great length his perceptions and anxieties about postwar America, particularly regarding the mediocrity, conformity, and pathology of White racism that he feels everywhere engulfs him. Perhaps he is most interesting when he attempts to describe to Miss Stein something of the New York literary scene, or the phenomenon of Father Divine, or the several connotations of the term "jive." One knows he feels more at ease with his famous correspondent when he suggests that *she* return to the United States and lecture White American artists on how obtuse they have been in overlooking the rich materials of Negro life.

Few of Wright's other correspondents received letters as carefully worked out as the ones he wrote to Gertrude Stein, although on occasion he would send off a long splendid letter if he felt the things he wanted to say merited thorough discussion. Thus, in a superbly written piece Wright examines and analyzes the assumptions of social welfare workers and finds these demoralizing and destructive to the clients they are presumably trying to help. It is a letter that persons involved in these issues today might still be well advised to read.[4] He writes another fine letter later on in the forties to a doctor who has requested his views on the psychology of Black Americans.[5]

Wright, however, reserves his most biting, tough, polemical prose for Burton Rascoe and David Cohn for their attacks on *Native Son* in the *Atlantic Monthly* and *American Mercury*. Wright's answers to these critics were published in the same periodicals, but a long letter he wrote to Mike Gold in May 1940 on a different kind of criticism that appeared in *The Daily Worker* was not published. Wright's response to Gold is far more inclusive and provocative, laying open the whole dilemma of the Black writer writing for both Black and White readers.

As revelations of the development of Wright's political, social, and racial views, the letters, as I have said earlier, are invaluable. In the main, although they pretty much reflect what he has written elsewhere, they illuminate certain areas of his thinking that are perhaps still misunderstood. For example, Wright's extended love affair and subsequent disillusionment with Communism is fairly well known (and is recorded again for us in these letters), but what is perhaps less well known is that even after his break with the Party, his early connection with Communism haunted him all his days. He was not so much bothered by the kind of insidious inquiries into his past associations by various red-hunting government agencies—about which he felt only contempt— but he was constantly made anxious that his genuine anti-Communist sentiments would be used by the Americans and to a lesser extent the British and French for their own nefarious purposes. On October 24, 1960 he wrote Oliver Swan—an associate of Paul Reynolds—that he would not participate in a Canadian Broadcasting Corporation program of contributors to Richard Grossman's book, *The God That Failed* (reminiscences of former Communists), because Canada is part of the British Commonwealth and Western world.

> The Western World must make up its mind as to whether it hates colored people more than it hates Communists or does it hate Communists more than it hates colored people. . . . If I take a strong line in public against the Communists and then find the West is making a deal with them [that is, white European Russia against colored China, Africa and Asia], it would place me in a very foolish position.

In some of his other letters to Margrit de Sabloniere he warns that the United States uses the non-Communist left to affect its anti-Communist campaign in Europe. He has especially in mind the Congress for Cultural Freedom whose publications, *Preuves* in France and *Encounter* in England, had printed some of Wright's pieces in previous years.

Conversely, he writes one of the sponsors of an African cultural festival that is scheduled to convene in London in 1959 that he cannot participate because the presence of some Communists may make it appear that he endorses their policies.[6] Toward the end of his life, however, Wright directed most of his ire toward Europe and the United States; he became more and more convinced that the West was incapable of throwing off its racist cast of mind and ingrown colonial attitudes. Moreover, the Western obsession with Communism was, he felt, a sure way of bringing about Communism's advent. Hence, in later letters to a variety of correspondents, Wright's anti-Communism was more than matched by a bitterness toward the West in general and America in particular—a bitterness which seems to have increased in direct relation to the number of years he remained away in exile.

The ambivalence Wright felt toward the West and Communism was to a certain extent carried over in his attitudes toward Africans and even Black Americans. Although he reaffirms in his letters that the best hope for Africa and Asia lies in an elite of Western-educated leaders who would draw the colored nations of the world away from the control of the West, he is much less sanguine about the prospects of immediate success than his books seem to indicate. He wrote Reynolds in 1954 that he was appalled by the squalor and corruption he found on the Gold Coast, and heard that other parts of Black Africa were far worse. He wrote Margrit de Sabloniere that even with the European powers physically gone from Africa, a passive colonial state of mind still persists among the inhabitants of former colonial areas.[7] The same is true even among the African intelligentsia he meets in Paris; he fears they have been snared by religion—particularly the Catholic church. He notes with anger, too, that on a recent visit to the offices of *Présence Africaine* with Dorothy Padmore he saw mainly White persons working there.[8] Wright's espousal of Black nationalism was not, however, intended as a racial concept. He tells Margrit de Sabloniere in an earlier letter that the title of his book, *Black Power*, means political and state power: "I did not have in mind any racial meaning."[9]

Wright's views about American Negroes were not unlike what he felt about Africans. In Paris, he observed to one correspondent, American Negroes brought with them the same mental attitudes they had been conditioned to in racist America, and it would be a long time before they were psychologically free.[10] He even believed that Black American intellectuals were controlled by their fears of what White America would find acceptable in their thinking. He would feel uneasy working for Negroes, he once wrote Reynolds, because, he implies, in attempting to be inoffensive to the White academic establishment they might attempt to curb his saying what he wants to say.[11] In a way, he wrote Margrit de Sabloniere in 1960, Negroes are more Western than the West, but because their culture rejects them, they do not know who they are.[12] "I wish somebody would tell me exactly *who* I am," he wrote in a letter six months before his death.[13]

One feels always that when Wright speaks of the West or Communism or American Negroes or the African elite or the colored masses the world over, he is really speaking about himself. Which is not to say that his conclusions are wrong or invalid for that reason, but which does suggest how complicated he was, how much he identified with in his lifetime, and how much he subsequently rejected in himself and in his world. As one looks over the expanse of letters, one is struck by his genuine compassion, his generosity in offering whatever help he could give to friends and even unknown persons in whose services to literature or to Negro culture or Black freedom he believed. But Wright's idealism was not untempered by a kind of hard-headed pragmatism. One notes, for example, that in 1940 when he was denouncing American capitalism in the Communist press, he wrote his agent, Paul Reynolds, in August of that year to buy him United States bonds.[14] Which is not to imply that Wright was a hypocrite (any more than George Bernard Shaw who despite his Fabian views exercised enormous capitalist acumen) but that Wright's Mississippi childhood and early days in Chicago left him with few romantic notions about poverty.

Regarding his deepest personal feelings about people, the letters do not tell us as much as we would like. He expresses a reserved affection for Margrit, and pride and love for his daughter, Julia (in a letter to Margrit) which one suspects he never declared outright. He was a shy man, perhaps afraid of his feelings. He feels warmly toward Paul Reynolds, and when he hears of the sudden death of his old friend, Ed Aswell, he is profoundly moved. Throughout his life, he maintains an interest and sense of financial responsibility toward his mother, brother, and aunt, but he says very little about them. Yet, for all his admirable qualities, Wright was not above occasional pettiness: he would sustain for years a grievance against someone whom he felt had betrayed him. Nor was he above a kind of smug provincialism— Catholics are depressing; Mexicans are careless of human life; as a general rule, Italians cannot be trusted; there are several other observations on the same level. Wright was obviously too sensitive and intelligent to believe the superficialities he would occasionally dash off, but it is interesting to note that he could dash them off. One is constantly reminded as well of his understandable but often unjustified suspicions of strangers, institutions, and even close friends. As a Southern Negro he had to scheme, plot, and intrigue to survive psychically—if not physically, but the toll was great, and he seemed to live always in a world of schemes, plots, and intrigues, a world which was sometimes real enough, judging from the level of CIA activities among Negroes and Whites he knew about in Paris. But when he writes a visiting American professor that he suspects that the British, French, and Americans were behind the abrupt cancellation of a lecture which he was supposed to deliver at the University of Nancy, one wonders: Was Wright really that much of a menace? [15] Similarly, in other letters he attributes the poor critical reception of some of his books and Ketti Fring's Broadway adaptation of his novel, *The Long Dream*, to ideological motives and political pressure—rather dubious reactions to critics who may have simply regarded some of his works as poor.

By far the most revealingly intimate view of Wright's state of mind may be found in the large number of letters he sent to Margrit de Sabloniere in the last years of his life. When one compares these letters—brooding, almost self-pitying, philosophical, groping, yet tough in their way as well—to some of his first letters to Southern childhood friends, Joe Brown and Essie Lee Ward, at the dawn of his success (*Uncle Tom's Children*, 1938), one is struck by the difference in tone. His early letters are proud, optimistic, almost swaggering. "I reckon you were rather amazed to hear that I'd gone to this great big city," he writes Joe Brown from New York. "Yes, I thought I was about ready to click, so I got together my duds and caught a bus." He goes on to tell about winning a Guggenheim prize for *Uncle Tom's Children*. "Buy a copy, boy! See what your old schoolmate and friend has done with the passing years!"[16] In the last year of his life, Wright was living alone, and quite literally sapped of strength by a recurring intestinal illness and its complications that had plagued him for years. Moreover, his finances were now so bad that he was reduced to writing texts for record companies. On November 24, 1960 he wrote Margrit de Sabloniere:

> Tonight I take the third million units of penicillin. It makes me weak and I feel dizzy. I keep to the house. I'll let you know how I progress. Thanks for your phone call. You are a dear. I am too weak to work now. Hell, I don't seem to have any luck this year at all.

It was his last unlucky year. Six days later he was seized with a heart attack and died.

Who was Wright? Did he really know himself? Poet, novelist, playwright, communist, existentialist, "international," revolutionary nationalist—but really always alone. His letters tell us that from the start he wanted to write for films, for radio; that he wanted to be a photographer, an actor, a war correspondent like Hemingway whom he envied; and toward the end of his life, he wanted to be editor of a crime magazine. Did he know really what he wanted? Somewhere he wrote, "The Negro is America's metaphor." Perhaps in his triumphs and defeats, in his generosity of spirit and in his failings, but above all in his dogged courage in trying to come to grips with himself and his world, Wright was the metaphor of all of us.

NOTES

1. Letter to Joe C. Brown (April 29, 1940).

2. Letter to Margrit de Sabloniere (April 22, 1956).

3. I am indebted to Ellen Wright (Wright's widow) for this information. At this writing, there is a strong possibility that several of Wright's letters to Ellen may be included in the collection.

4. Letter to Florence M. Seder (April 4, 1940).

5. Letter to Dr. Ruth Foster (June 3, 1945).

6. Letter to James Holness (July 7, 1959).

7. September 23, 1960. In part Wright blames this dependency on the tribal psychology they transferred to their White conquerors. As he states in the letter, he made this same point in *White Man, Listen!*

8. Letter to Margrit de Sabloniere (September 23, 1960).

9. Letter to Margrit de Sabloniere (June 9, 1955).

10. Letter to Paul Reynolds (March 2, 1959).

11. April 29, 1959. Wright's fears were not unjustified. Shortly afterwards, he wrote to John A. Davis, the executive secretary of the American Society of African Culture, requesting financial support for a proposed trip to French Africa to gather material for a new African book he was contemplating on the order of *Black Power*. Without committing himself, Davis responded that such sponsorship might harm the work in which AMSAC was interested. Wright then retorted (June 3, 1959) that under the circumstances he could not accept any aid from AMSAC:

> I've come to the conclusion that the prospect of doing "harm" would phychologically cripple me. . . . Certainly I'd not like to go there with the feeling that I'd have to inhibit myself in whatever I'd write.

On October 28, he wrote Reynolds that he had given up on the African trip—that the only money available was

> dirty money, that is, people who want me to go into Africa and spy on the Africans. In the first place, there's nothing in Africa to spy on and the thought of trying to fool naked, ignorant people sickens me. Some American Negroes are tough enough to do that, but I'm just not.

12. September 1, 1960.

13. April 26, 1960.

14. August 17, 1940.

15. Letter to Ernest Pick (April 27, 1960).

16. Letter to Joe C. Brown (March 1, 1938).

SOME LITERARY CONTACTS: AFRICAN, WEST INDIAN, AFRO-AMERICAN

Mercer A. Cook

The danger in this kind of presentation is that the speaker is likely to confuse influence with coincidence and may even be accused of seeing imitation where similar conditions have simply inspired similar literary treatment. I shall try to avoid both pitfalls. Let it be said at the outset that the dominant influence on African literature is Africa. Accepting the old definition of literature as the expression of a society, we cannot be surprised that Africans and persons of African descent, exposed to racism in places as distant as Mali, Martinique, Mississippi or Manhattan, Pretoria, Pittsburgh or Paris, should sometimes voice their protest in somewhat similar terms.

For influence to exist, there must be contact, and contacts are a two-way street. During the period of the Negro Renaissance, one point of contact was New York City, which had attracted such writers as W. E. B. DuBois, Walter White, James Weldon Johnson, Countee Cullen, and Langston Hughes. There, Alain Locke's *New Negro* was published in 1925. The following year *The Nation* carried an article by Langston Hughes, one paragraph of which has since been termed the manifesto of negritude:

> We younger Negro artists who create now intend to express our individual dark-skinned selves without fear or shame. If white people are pleased, we are glad. If they are not, it doesn't matter. We know that we are beautiful and ugly too. . . . If colored people are pleased, we are glad. If they are not, their displeasure doesn't matter either.[1]

By 1925, the time of my first visit to Paris, Hughes had already been there, and a young Martinican was translating some of his poems. Claude McKay had lived for a while in Marseilles. René Maran, whose novel, *Batouala*, had been awarded the Goncourt Prize in 1921, soon established contact with Alain Locke, Carter G. Woodson, Walter White, Rayford Logan, Countée Cullen, and other Black intellectuals visiting the French capital.

In the thirties, Maran continued to be the leading Black writer in France and to serve as a focal point for transatlantic contacts. His apartment on the rue Bonaparte attracted West Indian, French, and American Negro authors, as well as an occasional African student, notably Léopold Sédar Senghor.

But the circle widened. Through Maran, no doubt, Alain Locke met a young Martinican, Louis T. Achille, and persuaded him to come to teach at Howard University, where he remained for almost ten years. Achille, incidentally, wrote on Paul Laurence Dunbar for his *diplôme d'études supé-rieures* at the Sorbonne, and later pioneered in popularizing the spiritual in France. In 1931 Achille's cousin, Mlle. Paulette Nardal, founded the *Revue du Monde Noir,* a shortlived but useful periodical which published its articles both in French and in English. With its small nucleus of Blacks from several lands, it helped in some measure to break down the barrier between Martinicans, Africans, Haitians, and Afro-Americans.

Looking back on those early days, Senghor told a Howard University audience on September 28, 1966:

I am pleased to render homage here to the pioneer thinkers who lighted our path in the years 1930-35: Alain Locke, W. E. B. DuBois, Marcus Garvey, Carter G. Woodson. And also to pay well-deserved tribute to the poets whose works we translated and recited, and in whose footsteps we tried to follow: Claude McKay, Jean Toomer, Countée Cullen, James Weldon Johnson, Langston Hughes, Sterling Brown. I cannot forget the two magazines that we feverishly skimmed through: *The Crisis* and *Opportunity.* That was a time of fervor.

Through the years, Senghor continued to translate Black American poets, to quote them in essays, lectures, or casual conversation. In 1938 I was astonished by the facility with which he and Léon G. Damas—two of the three founders of the Negritude Movement—could quote our poets. At the time, the third founder of the Movement, Aimé Césaire, who invented the term negritude, was preparing a memoir on "The Theme of the South in Negro-American Literature." In one of Senghor's earliest important essays, "What the Black Man Has to Contribute"[2] (1939), he quoted Hughes, Cullen, McKay, and Lewis Alexander, and mentioned Jean Toomer in a footnote. In his lecture, "Negro-American Poetry"[3] (1950), he cited verses by Sterling Brown, Frank Marshall Davis, and Richard Wright once each; Claude McKay and Jean Toomer twice; Countée Cullen and James Weldon Johnson four times; Langston Hughes seven times.

Later in the fifties, as a member of the second Edgar Faure Government, one day Senghor telephoned his friend, Rudolph Aggrey, son of the famous Aggrey of Africa. Young Aggrey was then directing the USIA Cultural Center on the rue du Dragon. He wondered why Senghor would be calling a U. S. official on a day when the French Cabinet was about to fall. Nevertheless, he hurried to Senghor's apartment and found him seated calmly at his desk. "I've been translating this poem by Langston Hughes," said Senghor, "but I can't understand this word."

In 1965, addressing a group of aspiring young poets in Mali, Senghor cited the poem "Florida Road Workers" by Hughes as an example for them to follow. In all probability Senghor selected this work to prove that the deft touch of irony could be more effective than the propagandistic sledgehammer, and this ironic tone is clear in the following lines:

Sure, a road helps everybody
Rich folks ride
and I get to see 'em ride
I ain't never seen nobody
ride so fine before
Hey, Buddy, look
I'm makin' a road[4]

Another incident involving Senghor and Langston Hughes occurred in April 1966 during the Dakar Festival. Senghor sent me his translation of a poem on Ethiopia that Hughes had allegedly written thirty years earlier at the time of the Italian invasion. Planning to read the French version at a luncheon honoring His Imperial Majesty, Senghor asked me to show the translation to Langston for his approval. I immediately telephoned Hughes and read him the first few lines. "It's beautiful!" he exclaimed, "but unfortunately I didn't write it. I wish I had." That afternoon the president received Hughes and reminded him that the poem had been published in the magazine *Opportunity*. Only then did Langston recall that he had indeed written it as the lyric for a hymn that was featured at a pro-Ethiopian demonstration in New York City. Senghor's reading of the poem proved to be the highlight of the official luncheon attended by Emperor Haile Selassie, Senegalese officialdom, the diplomatic corps, and Langston Hughes.

I had always assumed that Hughes and Senghor had met in the thirties, on one of Langston's visits to Paris. To my surprise, I learned that theirs was purely a literary friendship until the early 1950s when Senghor first came to the States as a member of a French delegation to the United Nations:

123

In truth [Senghor wrote me on September 8, 1967] I did not meet Langston Hughes until very late, that is to say the first time I went to the United States . . . . On that occasion, I visited his home in Harlem several times. We fraternized immediately. Of course, I had read almost all his poems. I have always thought that, if Langston is not the greatest Negro-American poet . . . he was, without doubt, the most spontaneously Negro [poet]. In other words, he best fulfilled the notion I have of black cultural values, of Negritude. I believe, moreover, that Langston felt everything that linked us—Césaire, Damas, and me—to him.

Birago Diop, also Senegalese, was another member of the older generation of African writers in Paris who felt the impact of Hughes's genius. Like Maran, Damas, Césaire, Senghor, and Achille, this future author of the delightful *Contes d'Amadou Koumba* and *Nouveaux Contes d'Amadou Koumba*[5] joined the little group then publishing the *Revue du Monde Noir.* He decided to try out in French a rhythm that Langston had used in "Danse Africaine":

> The low beating of the tom-toms,
> The slow beating of the tom-toms,
> Low . . . slow
> Slow . . . low
> Stirs your blood.
> Dance![6]

Diop called his poem "Accords." Translated, it reads in part, as follows:

> Rough hands
> Scratch and scrape the tough soil

Tough hands, rough soil
Tough, rough
Rough, tough

Caresses please you
Farming appeases you
Tough soil, rough soil
Caresses of tough hands
Farming by rough hands
Tough, rough
Rough, tough

Birago Diop characterized that poem as an attempt "to try out the technique" of Langston Hughes's tom-toms. A somewhat similar experiment, inspired perhaps by Langston's use of the jazz idiom in poems like "The Weary Blues" and "Trumpet Player," was Martial Sinda's "Tam-tam, tam-tam-toi," which ends:

Trumpet, trumpet, O Armstrong, master of jazz
Trumpet, trumpet, to arouse all Black Africa
Trumpet, trumpet, to awaken sleeping Africa

O sweet trumpet of jazz
O rocking xylophone
O Congolese n'tsambi
O griots of my dear Dakar
O Zannie Amaya, dancer of Bangui
Rock us, rock us, keep on rocking us
Till the creation of a new Africa
New but always Black[7]

Similarly inspired, Guy Tirolien, of Guadeloupe, writes a poem called "Satchmo":

No
Don't tune out

> the hiccups, the sobs,
> the subtle glissandos
> the stridence, the insistence
> the cadence
> of the blues
> swinging, oh!
> to the trumpet of Satchmo[8]

Tirolien's poem continues for a few more stanzas, but perhaps this would be a good time to pause for a word of caution. Without detracting from Hughes's originality, we should not overlook the fact that, by his insistence on jazz, boogie woogie, drum and trumpet, Langston was simply going back to his roots. As Senghor has pointed out, the basic rhythm of an African poem is marked by percussion instruments or by the clapping of hands. In the preface to his anthology, *Poems from Black Africa,* Hughes remarks that the style of Senghor's poems is "really that of a chant." He then quotes his Senegalese friend:

> I insist that the poem is perfect only when it becomes a song: words and music at once. It is time to stop the decay of the modern world and especially the decay of poetry. Poetry must find its way back to its origins, to the times when it was sung and danced. As it was in Greece, above all in the Egypt of the Pharaohs. And as it still is today in black Africa.

It should be noted in passing that more than half of Senghor's poems specify the desired musical accompaniment: tom-tom, kora, balafon, jazz orchestra, and the like. As we said earlier, contacts are a two-way street.

Some of the most striking similarities in this writing reflect not so much the influence of one writer on another as relationships between Blacks and Whites in various countries. Thus Langston Hughes can write:

> I am the American heartbreak—
> Rock on which Freedom
> Stumps its toe—
> The great mistake
> That Jamestown
> Made long ago[9]

And, Bernard Dadié, of the Ivory Coast, can compare Harlem to "a wart on the face of New York," "a bone in the throat of New York, a cavity in its white teeth."[10]

Sterling Brown, in his poem "Strong Men," can report:

> Today they shout prohibition at you
> 'Thou shalt not this'
> 'Thou shalt not that'
> 'Reserved for whites only'
> You laugh
>
> One thing they cannot prohibit
> The strong men . . . coming on
> The strong men gittin' stronger
> Strong men . . . .
> Stronger . . . .[11]

Damas lists the following prohibitions in a love lyric:

> Attention/ Ici Danger / Déviation / Chasse gardée/
>   Terrain privé
> Domaine réservé/ Défense d'entrer / Ni chiens ni
>   nègres sur le gazon.[12]

127

In his novel, *Masters of the Dew,* Haitian Jacques Roumain strikes the same note:

> There's heavenly business and there's earthly business. They're two different things, not the same. The sky's the pastureland of the angels. They're fortunate—they don't have to worry about eating and drinking. Of course, they have black angels to do the heavy work—like washing out the clouds or cleaning off the sun after a storm—while the white angels just sing like nightingales all day long, or else blow on little trumpets. . . .[13]

In all these instances, the authors knew each other. Dadié had certainly read Langston Hughes in translation, if not in the original, and may have met him personally when he (Dadié) visited New York in 1963. L. G. Damas and Sterling Brown have been close friends for many years, at least since 1946. Cullen had met Roumain in New York, possibly in the early 1930s, and was much impressed by the talented Haitian. Consequently, there was contact between the authors of those six extracts, but I would be most reluctant to suggest that one directly influenced the other. Part of the Black experience, the passages quoted could have occurred to a gifted Negro writer anywhere. When the South African author Richard Rive, in a book of short stories dedicated to Langston Hughes, relates "The Return," imagining Christ revisiting the earth as a colored man and being rejected by a South African church for whites, we are first tempted to think of "Not for Publication," the well-known poem in which Hughes speculates on the racial hardships of a Black Christ in the U.S.A.

Remembering Countee Cullen's title, *The Black Christ,* and a line or two from his poem "Heritage," where he fashions "dark gods too"; reading the Ghanaian poet Francis Ernest Kobina Parkes's: "Our God is powerful, All-powerful and black"; recalling these and other examples in Negro poetry and Negro life, I am quite ready to believe that "The Return" would still have been written even if "Not for Publication" had lived up to its title.

There are, of course, works in which a direct reference to a title or an author obviously indicates influence or at least contact. In his magnificent poem "New York," Senghor mentions *God's Trombones* and ends with lines vaguely reminiscent of the style used by James Weldon Johnson in those Negro sermons:

But it is enough to open your eyes to the April
    rainbow
and your ears, above all your ears, to God who
    with the laugh
of a saxophone created heaven and earth in six
    days
And on the seventh day he slept the great sleep of
    the Negro. [14]

Joseph Zobel, of Martinique, speaks flatteringly of Claude McKay's *Banjo* in his prize-winning novel, *La Rue Cases-Nègres.* Ousmane Socé, of Senegal, also mentions *Banjo* in his *Mirages de Paris.* Tchicaya U Tam'si, of Congo Brazzaville, speaks in his poem, *Epitomé,* of "singing the Weary Blues" (either the poet or his printer misspells "Weary" as "Warry").

129

Contacts, literary or personal, with Haiti were more numerous and deserve a separate paragraph. James Weldon Johnson, Langston Hughes, Rayford Logan, Alain Locke, W. E. B. DuBois, and others had visited the Black republic between 1920 and 1950 and most of them had written about it. *La Revue Indigène,* founded in 1927 by a group of young Haitians including Jacques Roumain, told its readers about the new Negro writing in the United States. Five years later the first two issues of Jacques Antoine's *La Relève* carried an article, "La Renaissance nègre des Etats-Unis," by Dr. Jean Price-Mars, who has been called "the Father of Negritude." On October 20, 1931, *Haiti-Journal* published a poem by Jacques Roumain which paid tribute to Langston Hughes as poet and Black American.[15] Interestingly enough, it was in Haiti that what Langston called "the first book about me in any language," *Langston Hughes: Un chant nouveau,* by Dr. René Piquion, was published in 1940.

These contacts resulted not so much in imitation as in a broadened perspective, a growing appreciation for the values of the Black world, a lessening of an inferiority complex planted deep by centuries of brainwashing and assorted tortures. After all, it was about time for someone to suggest that Black Beauty did not have to be a horse.

One of the most effective and influential illustrations of this new attitude was Claude McKay's *Banjo.* Published in 1928, translated into French the following year, this novel created a sensation among French-speaking African and West Indian intellectuals. Basically, it urged the Black man to be himself—"without fear or shame," as Langston Hughes had insisted in his 1926 manifesto—and it did so with artistry and humor. Knocking around on the docks of Marseilles, the hero decided to form a small combo as a means of making a little money:

> "Banjo! That's what you play?" exclaimed Goosey.
>
> "Sure that's what I play," replied Banjo. "Don't you like it?"
>
> "No. Banjo is bondage. It's the instrument of slavery. Banjo is Dixie. The Dixie of the land of cotton and massa and missus and black mammy. We colored folks have got to get away from all that in these enlightened, progressive days. Let us play piano and violin, harp and flute. Let the white folks play the banjo if they want to keep on remembering all the black Joes singing and the hell they made them live in."
>
> "That ain't got nothing to do with me . . . ," replied Banjo. "I play that theah instrument becaz I likes it. I don't play no black Joe hymns. I play lively tunes. All that you talking bout slavery and bondage ain't got nothin to do with our starting up a li'l orchestry." [16]

Now, if you will hold on to that banjo for a moment, I shall read part of L. G. Damas's poem "Hoquet," first published in 1937:

> In vain I drank seven mouthfuls of water
> three or four times in twenty-four hours
> my childhood returns
> in a hiccup shaking up

my instinct
like the cop the robber

Disaster
tell me of the disaster
tell me about it

. . . .

Disaster
tell me of the disaster
tell me about it

My mother wanting a son very do
very re/ very mi/ very fa/ very sol/ very la/ very ti
very do/ re mi fa/ sol la ti/do
I heard you missed your violin lesson
A banjo? you say a banjo? what are you saying?
a banjo? are you really saying banjo?
No sir! here we shall tolerate
neither ban
nor jo
    nor gui
    nor tar
Mulattoes don't do that
Leave that to *Negroes.* [17]

Even if the original impetus came from McKay, it tied in with memories of Damas's childhood in Cayenne and Fort-de-France closely enough to inspire a poem that is typically, authentically, and exclusively Damas.

After World War II the contacts became more frequent. To cite only a few of the most notable, *Présence Africaine* began publication in 1947, with Richard Wright a member of its *Comité de Patronage,* along with Gide, Camus, Sartre, Paul

Hazoumé (of Dahomey), and several others. Almost immediately its resourceful editor, Alioune Diop, attracted collaborators from Africa, the Americas, and Europe, people of different political and religious persuasion. In 1948 James Baldwin moved to Paris; subsequently Chester Himes arrived. In 1951 sociologist E. Franklin Frazier came over to begin a two-year assignment with UNESCO. Published in Paris before being brought out in this country, his *Bourgeoisie noire* reported some characteristics in the Black American middle class that Frantz Fanon had detected in his West Indian congeners in *Peau noire, masques blancs.*

Wright's presence provided tremendous stimulus to aspiring African and West Indian writers in Paris. Here was a successful Black novelist who had already produced several works—*Native Son, Black Boy, Uncle Tom's Children*—that had won international acclaim. He became a standard of comparison, something of an ideal. In the preface of Ousmane Socé's *Karim* (1948 edition), French colonial administrator Robert Delavignette was pleased to note that this Senegalese novel lacked the bitterness of Wright's *Black Boy.* At the other extreme, Cameroonian novelist Mongo Beti criticized Camara Laye, of Guinea, for not making his *Enfant noir* (1953) more militant in the manner of Wright's autobiography. On the jacket of Sembène Ousmane's second novel, *O Pays, mon beau peuple* (1958), his publisher asked: "Could he be a second Richard Wright?" This because Sembène's first novel, *Le Docker noir* (1956), bore a rather superficial resemblance to *Native Son,* especially in the lawyer's defense of the African accused of murdering a

133

French woman. [Some years later in an interview published in Dakar, Sembène Ousmane said that Jacques Roumain had influenced him more. As a matter of fact, the impact of *Masters of the Dew* on *O Pays, mon beau peuple* is more pronounced than that of *Native Son* on *Le Docker noir.*] Nevertheless, it would be difficult to overemphasize the importance of Wright's contribution during the hectic 1950s when so much of Africa stood on the threshold of independence. This influence was not restricted to the novel. His trip to the Gold Coast (Ghana) resulted in a book that aroused mixed reactions in some Africans, but his title, *Black Power*, seems likely to last.

With the coming of the nineteen sixties, African independence, the availability of many African authors in inexpensive editions, conferences which have brought African writers to our shores, art festivals in Dakar and Algiers, visits to Africa by Afro-American leaders—all resulted in an increased awareness of what was being said, done, and written on that continent. A few weeks ago I quoted three famous lines by Aimé Césaire to a class. My students did not have the text as we had not yet reached Césaire in the course. After class a young Afro-American came up to ask the meaning of a word (kai'lcédrat) which occurs in the line preceding those I had quoted. This could hardly have happened ten or fifteen years ago, when many of our youngsters could not even identify W. E. B. DuBois. In this connection, when Langston Hughes published *Ask Your Mama* in 1961, very few of our young people could have recognized the names in this line: ALIOUNE AIME SEDAR

SIPS HIS NEGRITUDE—not so today, thanks to the proliferation of courses in African literature, translations, anthologies, and articles, not to mention Baldwin's account of the 1956 *Présence Africaine* Paris Conference and Eldridge Cleaver's glowing tribute to Aimé Césaire in *Soul on Ice,* or the numerous references in Fanon.

As a result, traffic on our two-way street has become heavier and heavier. Let me conclude with two recent examples, chosen more or less at random. The first comes from Bob Kaufman's *Solitudes crowded with loneliness* (1965). I quote a part of his poem "Benediction":

> America, I forgive you . . . I forgive you
> Nailing black Jesus to an imported cross
> Every six weeks in Dawson, Georgia
> America, I forgive you . . . I forgive you
> Burning Japanese babies defensively
> I realize how necessary it was.
> Your ancestor had beautiful thoughts in his brain
> His descendants are experts in real estate.
> Your generals have mushrooming visions.
> Every day your people get more and more
> Cars, televisions, sickness, death dreams.
> You must have been great
> Alive.[18]

Similarly Senghor had written seventeen years earlier in his "Prayer for Peace":

> Lord God, forgive white Europe.
> It is true, Lord, that for four enlightened centuries,
>   she has scattered the baying and slaver of her
>   mastiffs over my lands

And the Christians, forsaking Thy light and the
gentleness of Thy heart
Have lit their camp fires with my parchments,
tortured my disciples, deported my doctors
and masters of science.

. . . .

Lord, forgive them who turned the Askia into
maquisards, my princes into sergeant-majors
My household servants into 'boys,' my peasants
into wage-earners, my people into a working
class.
For Thou must forgive those who have hunted my
children like wild elephants,
And broken them in with whips, have made them
the blacks hands of those whose hands were
white. [19]

Perhaps the analogy here means simply that both our
poets have forgiving natures and that Europe and America are
both "standing in the need of prayer." Again, in Senghor's
words, "Who [but the Black man] would teach rhythm to a
dead world of machines and guns?"

And now for our final example, David Diop's "Le
Temps du martyr," first published in 1948 and somewhat
reminiscent of the earlier style of Langston Hughes:

The white man killed my father
My father was proud
The white man raped my mother
My mother was beautiful
The white man bent my brother under the highway
sun

My brother was strong
The white man turned toward me
His hands red with black blood
And, in the voice of a master:
"Hey, boy! bring me a whiskey, a napkin, and some
     water!" [20]

Here is a poem powerful in its stark portrayal of four tragedies, compressed into ten short lines bristling with anger all the more ominous because unexpressed. One thinks perhaps of Langston's "Cross" or "Brass Spittoons":

Clean the spittoons, boy.

. . . .

Hey, boy!
A nickel,
A dime,
A dollar,
Two dollars a day
     Hey, boy! [21]

In a recent anthology, *Black Fire*, there is a poem by Lance Jeffers which starts out in a style reminiscent of Aimé Césaire and picks up David Diop along the way:

My blackness is the beauty of this land,
my blackness,
tender and strong, wounded and wise.
I, drawling black grandmother, smile muscular and sweet,
unstraightened white hair soon to grow in earth,
work-thickened hand thoughtful and gentle on grandson's head
my heart is bloody-razored by a million memories' thrall,

137

remembering the crooked-necked cracker who
    spat on my naked body,
remembering the splintering of my son's spirit
    because he remembered to be proud
remembering the tragic eyes in my daughter's
    dark face when she learned her color's
    meaning
and my own dark rage a rusty knife with teeth to
    gnaw my bowels,
my agony ripped loose by anguished shouts in
    Sunday's humble church,
my agony rainbowed to ecstacy when my feet
    oversoared Montgomery's slime,
ah, this hurt, this hate, this ecstacy before I die,
and all my love a strong cathedral!
My blackness is the beauty of this land![22]

Thus we have come full circle, from the Afro-American
poets of the Negro Renaissance to the West Indian and
African writers of the Negritude Movement and back again.
Our examples of possible influence, or at least of contact,
have been selected mostly from the area of Negro-American
and black Francophone works because that is primarily
where your speaker has been looking for the past three
decades. I surmise that future research will reveal traffic
almost as congested—and moving in both directions—between
Black American and African literature in English.

NOTES

1. Langston Hughes, "The Negro Writer and the Racial Mountain," reprinted in *Black Expression: Essays by and about Black Americans in the Creative Arts* ed. Addison Gayle, Jr. (New York: Weybright and Talley, 1969), p. 263.

2. Leopold S. Senghor, "What the Black Man Has to Contribute," in *L'Homme de couleur* (Paris: Plon, 1939), pp. 292-314.

3. Senghor, *Liberté I: Négritude et humanisme* (Paris: Seuil, 1964), pp. 104-121.

4. Hughes, "Florida Road Workers," in *The Panther and the Lash: Poems of Our Times* (New York: Alfred A. Knopf, 1969), p. 41.

5. Birago Diop, *Contes d'Amadou Koumba* (Paris: Fasquelle, 1947); and *Nouveaux Contes d'Amadou Koumba* (Paris: Présence Africaine, 1958).

6. Hughes, "Danse Africaine," in *Selected Poems* (New York: Alfred Knopf, 1959), p. 7.

7. Martial Sinda, *Premier Chant du départ* (Paris: Seghers, 1956), p. 27.

8. Guy Tirolien, *Balles d'or* (Paris: Présence Africaine, 1960), p. 63.

9. Hughes, "I Am the American Heartbreak," in *The Panther and the Lash* (p. 25).

10. Bernard Dadié, *Hommes de tous les continents* (Paris: Présence Africaine, 1965).

11. Sterling Brown, *Negro Caravan,* eds. Sterling Brown, Arthur P. Davis, and Ulysses Lee (New York: Dryden Press, 1941), p. 391.

12. L.G. Damas, *Névralgies* (Paris: Présence Africaine, n.d.), p. 33.

13. Jacques Roumain, *Masters of the Dew,* trans. Langston Hughes and Mercer Cook (New York: Reynal and Hitchcock, 1947), p. 23.

Mercer A. Cook

14. Senghor, *Poèmes* (Paris: Seuil, 1964), p. 117.
15. Edna W. Underwood, *The Poets of Haiti: 1782-1934* (Portland, Me.: Mosher Press, 1934), pp. 66-67. I am grateful to Maurice A. Lubin for the text and date of publication of the original version.
16. Claude McKay, *Banjo* (New York: Harper, 1928), p. 90.
17. Damas, *Pigments* (Paris: Présence Africaine, 1962), pp. 33-36.
18. Bob Kaufman, "Benediction," in *The Poetry of the Negro 1746-1970*, eds. Langston Hughes and Arna Bontemps, rev. ed. (New York: Doubleday, 1970), p. 412.
19. Senghor, *Poèmes* (p. 93). I quote from Senghor, Selected Poem, trans. John Reed and Clive Wake (New York: Atheneum, 1964), pp. 48-49.
20. David Diop, *Coups de pilon* (Paris: Présence Africaine, 1961), p. 34.
21. Hughes, "Brass Spittoons," in *The Book of American Negro Poetry*, ed. James Weldon Johnson, Harbrace Paperbound Library ed. (New York: Harcourt, Brace, and World, 1959), pp. 234-235.
22. LeRoi Jones and Larry Neal eds. *Black Fire: An Anthology of Afro-American Writing* (New York: Morrow, 1968, p. 273.

140

DIALECT IN WEST INDIAN LITERATURE

Ismith Khan

When we speak of "West Indian writing," "Black writing," or the writing of any subculture, some definition as well as distinction should be made, if only for the sake of communication. If we consider the terms West Indian writing, Black writing, Jewish writing, Southern writing, one can readily see that these terms could refer to a writer who writes about that subculture, or a writer who is himself a member of that subculture and writes about it. One could, however, take the extreme position and insist that a piece of writing meet the aesthetic requirements without any further considerations.

141

The luxury of those idealists who insist that they write for themselves cannot be afforded by writers whose milieu is essentially a subculture. One finds in one work or another that one has to come to grips with the limitations of language, and further, one has to concede that one is unwittingly addressing oneself to a particular audience when one chooses characters and incidents, or as some writers prefer to put it, when some character or incident chooses the writer.

It is for this reason that I have chosen to speak about language and dialect, their uses, limitations, and more specifically the manner in which they shape and direct the conception of a piece of writing. Later on I shall discuss how this relates to the artist and his role in society.

There is no doubt in my mind that somewhere along the line in the conception or the gestation of a novel, play, poem, or short story, the piece begins to write itself. The locale, the incident, and the principals are already well formed in the writer's mind, and since we are dealing with words, speech, language, all of the indications of those characters in their particular roles must come from within the limits of those characters, their actions, and their possibilities. If the writer exceeds or minimizes these limits, an incomplete characterization or an unconvincing one results.

The dialect of "Simple Speaks his Mind" permits Langston Hughes a great amount of leeway, yet Simple's language cannot go beyond certain limits, nor for that matter can his thoughts go out of bounds. There must be a congruence along which the writer walks precariously if he is to be convincing. The same writer who may well have the highest grammatical standards at his fingertips, the same writer who may have a great many deep philosophical thoughts knows that they may not fit into his story, that to stray from the limits he has set for himself by choosing his particular milieu would be to make of his work something superficial and paper thin.

Now this may well seem like a simple task. One merely decides, and having made one's choice, one goes on to write with the consistency of language which is in keeping with character and incident, but the impact of uniqueness of expression in dialect is so strong, its exactness of meaning so singular, that the statements or thoughts of a character coming from any subculture cannot bear translation into plain straightforward Anglo-Saxon. Does one go as far afield as Richard Wright in the search for new spellings which would render the exactness of a Black Southerner's speech? Does one try for a common denominator as I believe Alan Paton did in *Cry the Beloved Country?"* Should the writer begin to scurry about when a publisher wishes to do his book but then suggests that the dialogue, the dialect, is going to slow up the reader? Should the writer try at the other extreme to prune his prose so that he gets just the flavor of his character's speech with a minimum of difficulty for the reader? Of course it is the writer's choice in the end, but what terrible and unfortunate choices.

I should now like to consider two examples of West Indian writing. The first is an extract from a short story, "La Divine Pastors," by C. L. R. James, set in Trinidad and published in 1928. The reader will note that although the content of the story is rich in local lore, it nonetheless foregoes the usage of West Indian language and dialect.

Of my own belief in this story I shall say nothing. What I have done is to put it down as far as possible just as it was told to me, in my own style, but with no addition to or subtraction from the essential facts.

Anita Perez lived with her mother at Bende l'Este Road, just at the corner where North Trace joins the Main Road. She had one earthly aim. She considered it her duty to be married as quickly as possible, first because in that retired spot it marked the sweet perfection of a woman's existence, and secondly, because feminine youth and beauty, if they exist, fade early in the hard work on the cocoa plantations. Every morning of the week, Sunday excepted, she banded down her hair, and donned a skirt which reached to her knees, not with any pretensions to fashion but so that from seven till five she might pick cocoa, or cut cocoa, or dry cocoa or in some other way assist in the working of Mr. Kayle Smith's cocoa estate. She did this for thirty cents a day, and did it uncomplainingly, because her mother and father had done it before her, and had thriven on it. On Sundays she dressed herself in one of her few dresses, put on a little gold chain, her only ornament, and went to Mass. She had no thought of woman's rights, nor any Ibsenic theories of morality. All she knew was that it was her duty to get married, when, if she was lucky, this hard life in the cocoa would cease.

Every night for the past two years Sebastian
Montagnio came down from his four-roomed mansion, half a mile up the trace, and spent about an
hour, sometimes much more, with the Perez
family. Always, he sat on a bench by the door,
rolling cheap cigarettes and half-hiding himself in
smoke. He was not fair to outward view but yet
Anita loved him. Frequently half an hour would
elapse without a word from either, she knitting or
sewing steadily, Sebastian watching her con-
tentedly and Mrs. Perez sitting on the ground just
outside the door, smoking one of Sebastian's
cigarettes and carrying on a ceaseless monologue in
the local patois. Always when Sebastian left, the
good woman rated Anita for not being kinder to
him. Sebastian owned a few acres of cocoa and a
large provision garden, and Mrs. Perez had an idea
that Anita's marriage would mean relief from the
cocoa-work, not only for Anita but also for her.

Anita herself said nothing. She was not the talking
kind. At much expense and trouble, Sebastian sent
her a greeting card each Christmas. On them were
beautiful words which Anita spelt through so often
that she got to know them by heart. Otherwise,
nothing passed between the two. That he loved no
one else she was sure. It was a great consolation;
but did he love her? Or was it only because his
home was dull and lonely, and theirs was just at
the corner that he came down every night?[1]

The second example is from "Shadows Move in the
Brittania Bar," an unpublished short story of my own written
in 1965. Again, the reader will note that the story deals with

Ismith Khan

local lore, but is presented with all of the color and richness
of language and dialect, without which its total impact would
be meaningless.

> The time that I talkin bout, all yuh fellers didn't
> dream to born yet. Dem was the old time days.
> People uses to have a kind of belief in dem days, a
> respec for all what they see happen with they own
> two eye. What I mean to say is that things does still
> happen, but is people, like all yuh young fellers, is
> people who blind, they eye shut, it half close. But
> it have something. Where? Up in the sky! inside
> your belly! a man! God! It have something!

> In dem days it didn't have so much motor car to
> jam up the road. Port-of-Spain wasn't pack up with
> so much people. Trinidad? Hm! Dis Island uses to
> be different in dem times, boy, different. People
> uses to work hard hard hard! Not like nowadays,
> all you could hear is Independence, Federation,
> Hilton Hotel . . . . People askin me if I ent see how
> the Town change up. "Look how we have six story
> sky scraper . . . look how we have elevator in the
> department store, look how we have Woolworth 5
> & 10." I have to laugh because I ent see nothin
> change. People in Trinidad stop the same way . . .
> chupid! It have something and I know because I
> see with my own two eye.

> One o'clock, two o'clock we leavin dem far far
> places in the bush to reach Port-of-Spain before
> day-clean. Nobody on the road. And Dark? Pitch
> black! All you have is your little hurricane lantern
> prop up on top your cart, and it loaded down with
> coals. But what good dat lamp is? Is for police nuh

146

. . . for them not to give you a case, lock you up for drivin without light. But where you go find police at that hour? Dem rascals gone to catch a sleep somewhere too.

O-ho . . . so you think that is thief I talkin bout? What thief want to hold up a coal man? Is joke you makin'. Everybody know that a coal man ent have a cent with he when he goin in to town. Not thief . . . no, no. Not living people. Dem is not what I talkin' bout . . . something else. It have people who could do something to you, and all you young fellars can't see because you ent believe. That is why you ent have the respect what we have for them things. It have to have something . . . dis world ent make out from nothin . . . somebody . . . something does make it turn round, and I see things that make me know that . . . and if I ain't see dem, then my name ent Sookoo and I is a blasted liar so help me God. Ah say me name ent Sookoo and God lick me down wid a big-stone if I lie! I know what I talkin bout and if I lie I die.

I see enough thing to make your blood crawl . . . and that ent all. You remember it had a fellar name Mehal? Remember how he uses to walk miles doin up he hand and foot like if he drivin a motor car? The man uses to walk quite from Tunapuna all the way through San Juan and Curepe shiftin gear and blowing horn . . . You think is mad he mad? He whole family the same way too you know. Is somebody who make him get so. He had a sister who uses to crawl on she hand and foot like a dog too. I tellin you is something bad dat family gone and do and somebody make them come so.

You livin in Trinidad so long and you never hear
bout Obeah? You ent see because you ent believe.
Is your own bad-luck if you ent want to listen to
people what see for theyself. But I know it have
something outside there boys. Something big and
strong, and I see it already.

The writer of fiction has much greater leeway than the
playwright in that fiction has room for great passages of
narrative in which the writer can move some distance away
from the particular speech patterns of his characters. The
narrative can take the form of the erudite, the detached, the
lyrical; or, as has been the case with some writers, some
attempt has been made to keep the distance at a minimum
and their narrative has been pitched as close as possible to the
inner experience of their characters and their milieux. Put
another way, the writer through the narrative, attempts to use
the form and expression of his characters' innermost
thoughts, in the *kind* of language that such a character would
normally, realistically employ to express his thoughts.

A recent play, *Dream On Monkey Mountain* written by
the West Indian Derek Walcott is worth considering at this
point. In the first place, the playwright is a well established
poet, and one senses his frustration with the dramatic form.
Not satisfied with having his characters "speak their lines"
the playwright goes out of the way to squeeze in passages of
monologue, which although beautiful in themselves as
poetry, are nonetheless lines which could not have been
spoken by the characters in his play. The simplicity of their
lives, and the remoteness of their village provide two sides:
one which gives the writer all of the wealth of their local

color, beliefs, and dramatic possibilities, but at the same time, restricts the writer's choice. None of his characters could possibly speak with the sophistication, the erudition, and the poetry which are emulations of British standards. Since the writer is loathe to cut things out or throw things away, he twists, bends, and forces extraneous elements into the body of his work—he must have those lines even though they are in a language, meter, and rhythm totally alien to his characters and their lives.

It would be unfair to say that the play was a failure, because despite problems of this kind, there is much which can be readily understood and appreciated. Had the writer gone to the extreme end of the spectrum of West Indian dialect, it is doubtful that as much of the play would have been understood by American or English audiences. Yet, it is just this cry which has shot up with the coming of Independence to the area, a cry for something, anything, which is autonomous, nationalistic, home-grown; since there is no language besides English with such varying amounts of pidgin, the writer has pigeonholed himself before he even begins.

Similarly, in another play, *No Place to Be Somebody*, by the Black American playwright, Charles Gordone, the audience knows from the time the curtain goes up that Mr. Gordone is a poet working in the form of the drama. Here again, there are long monologues whose language and content could not possibly have been attributed to the dramatic incidents. The playwright therefore has them spoken by one of the characters as a kind of chorus, or stage setting, before the action and the interrelationships between the characters begin. Unlike the West Indian play, Mr. Gordone manages to deliver the monologue with all of the color and content of a Black man speaking with all his particular rhythms and pronunciations of English. Although they are monologues, their strength, their beauty derive from the authenticity and the idiom, the language and the dialect of the characters' lives. As the drama unfolds, the audience is not jarred or surprised by shifts in language or by dialect in the monologues. The play is a well balanced piece of work which remains faithful to its characters' dialect and language.

But how does this work in fiction, where the reader, the audience, does not have the actors' advantage of knowing the dialect and speaking it with perfection? One may well ask, what's wrong with the dialect novel, and why not a West Indian dialect novel? Most visitors to the Caribbean are enchanted with the particular lilt and music of its dialect, yet writers from the area work its dialect over a vast spectrum, some using none whatsoever, others going overboard, writing in such extreme forms that even a West Indian from a neighboring island would find it difficult to follow. Dialect varies so from one island to another that one West Indian, after a few sentences, can tell exactly from which island another West Indian comes. The problems of comprehension are multiplied if the readers or listeners are strangers to the area, and it is just this foreign readership that West Indian writers depend upon, since the area's readership is not only small, but vastly indifferent to local works.

"Who needs to go to a play by a West Indian, or read one of his books when all one has to do is go out on the streets" is the common cry of the West Indian. Or as others put it, "That's the sort of thing that the English and Americans like; it's all right for them." Still others feel that to portray the Caribbean in its original speech and dialect is to belittle the area; they would much prefer to see its writers represent them as an educated, sophisticated, White, Anglo-Saxon world that, they feel, would not degrade and cause others to look down on West Indian life. The artist, however, instinctively knows the basic fibre of his background and carries on as best he can, and one can only hope that the day will come when most West Indians will see that their own version of the English language has singular characteristics which are not only beautiful but necessary to the depiction of any West Indian work.

But the answer to the question, "Why not a West Indian dialect novel?" does not end here, for although there are admirers of the "dialect novel," their numbers are small. And while it is true, if one thinks of *Catcher in the Rye* as a dialect novel, its readership is not small, one should also look at another dialect novel, Roth's *Call It Sleep*, which went completely unnoticed at its original publication, and which when reissued many years later had much greater success— events I have not myself understood. Even so, it has been said that it was near impossible to read.

It has been argued that Southern American writers fare well enough in their readership both North and South, as well as internationally. If that is so, then why is it not so with West Indian dialect? In the first place, I do not know of many Southern novels written completely in Southern dialect. In the second place, because of communications media, the mobility of Americans, films and television, the average American is not totally unfamiliar with Southern accent and dialect. If anything, writers like Carson McCullers, Flannery O'Conner, and Truman Capote have brought a refreshing atmosphere to the reader's mind because of preconditioned experience and exposure to the American South; however, the kind of preparation which would make for the fullest grasp of meaning and emotional commitment does not exist for the tones and rhythms, the singular words, with their singular meanings, of West Indian dialect.

There is, I am certain, in the "bottom drawer" of more than one West Indian writer, *that* dialect novel which we have all wanted to write, and which will remain in the bottom drawer if only because of discouragement from the publishing world. I have in my bottom drawer, not a novel, but a short story in complete West Indian dialect, but the reactions I have had from editors and publishers were enough to dampen my enthusiasm. I could not bring myself to put in a year's work on a full-length, dialect novel because no writer writes for the bottom drawer.

At this point in time, it is all too clear that music, painting, sculpture, and the written and spoken word have all worked together in the formation of West European culture. Similarly, in Indian history, the Vedas, the religious texts, the Ragas in music, and the dance are all inextricably bound together. The emerging artist has a definition of his role within that cultural heritage, for within it lies all of the hopes, beliefs, superstitions, myths, and it is to this fount that the artist journeys from time to time in order to redefine, to vivify, to establish his position in the universe. This definition has always been the function of art and artistic creations.

In all societies, the artist is an embodiment of his culture and society. He functions within the framework of his heritage, and through his labors, he adds, enriches, and further defines that background. The picture is an entirely different one for the West Indian, as it is for the American Black, and for similar reasons. No one living in the West Indies is indigenous to the area. By the time its current inhabitants arrived, those pre-Columbian dwellers were extinct. Our cities, parks, public buildings, places of worship have nothing whatever to do with the Caribs and the Arawaks; they are bits and scraps of Spain, England, Scotland, Wales, and Ireland all held together by the English language. The West Indian artist, therefore, came to define himself, not in terms of his original ancestry, not in terms of the people indigenous to his geography, but in terms of something else and the way in which he sees himself in relation to that something else. Hence, we have had Black men writing in White tongues, and if I may say so, not without pride, praise, and general admiration. To be Black, and to be able to write poems considered comparable to Byron, Keats, or Shelley was truly admirable. We saluted these Black men seated on the same podium with the White governor, and secretly as we stood at attention in the sun, we hoped that one day we too would gain the respect and admiration that he, that Black man, was obviously enjoying, having learnt to emulate word, gesture, and I daresay emotional make-up of the White man.

The expression, "Black is beautiful" is a shockingly recent one. One cannot help but ask oneself just what Blacks thought themselves to be before. There is a good possibility that that image was shaped by the attempt to define Black in terms of the great White world. Any such definition must demand some form of emulation of something other than oneself, other than one's own intrinsic possibilities and potentialities. The expression "Black is beautiful" is a clear statement which finally suggests some kind of autonomy, some kind of coming to terms with oneself for what one is, recognizing intrinsic worth and beauty, and shaking off any attempt to emulate the codes and standards of any group or force, no matter what its size or function.

In the West Indies, one was taught to emulate English as the English wrote it and spoke it. If one expected to excel in the world of the literary, one had to do so in those terms. There was no body of West Indian literature, say twenty years ago, and now that there is, it is not difficult to see some of the most impressive works come from those writers who have portrayed their characters in their singular milieu with their own language and particular dialect. Unfortunately, there is still some ambivalence on the question of language and dialect. We have been told in innumerable studies by social scientists that there is a direct relationship between

154

social and economic status, and language and dialect. While this may indeed be so, there is a naive implication which suggests that if one were to change one's usage of language and dialect, one could also improve one's social and economic status.

The task of the artist is not the same as that of the cricketer or the soccer player, or anyone in competitive sports. It is one thing to learn to play English sports so that one can compete with the other man and play as good a game if not better. When one writes about one's culture and society, there is nothing competitive about it; unlike competitive sports, one does not have to follow the rules of the other man, hoping to be favorably compared. One is dealing with something organic and autonomous, an end in itself as all works of art must ultimately be.

The calypso for example was sung not only in dialect, but also in odds and ends of Patois, with some African words and other words which had meaning to the slave and indentured worker only. They were usually jibes at the masters and overseers who were within earshot but who could not and did not understand what was being said about them. Later on, calypsos attacked and lampooned local scandal, or they expressed the innermost feelings of the people on some local happening or their reactions to some international issue.

But witness what has happened to the form as it became a product for the vast tourist industry of the area. The content has had to change, and with it its intrinsic language and dialect. It is no longer a form of protest or jibe, but one

155

of pandering to foreign tastes which clearly does not say anything about our own domestic situation; it does not, as it once did, comment upon, redefine, and vivify the milieu from which it was born. One of the most galling experiences to a West Indian is to hear the players of the steel drum beating out "The Star-Spangled Banner" on their instruments. Most of the old-time calypsonians are gone, but their ballads survive to this day, and their survival over time is not mere chance; one has only to consider the themes they handled, to see how this art form touched upon the vital issues and needs of the day while most of today's compositions come and go without ever achieving any more distinction than being mere entertainment.

Cultural heritage is lost to West Indians, just as it is to Black Americans because language, the fundamental carrier of culture and tradition, is lost. One finds, therefore, a great many works which for want of a better description can be categorized as *The Return of the Native* in search of his roots, his heritage, his identity. And while some have made that journey, the body of their work remains essentially in the form of the "quest." I do not wish to underestimate this quest, because it is essential for a people, an individual, to have some sense of identity, broken though it may be by two or three centuries.

It is then clear that we are not merely speaking of language, but the loss of language, and of heritage, its toll, and the search for identity; one can only wonder just how well, through the imposition of a superstructure of English or any other language for that matter, the expatriate, uprooted

156

or oppressed, can find his way to any kind of definition of himself. There are those in the West Indies who face this brick wall with a childlike optimism. They take the view that the artist under these circumstances is completely unfettered by tradition, and is about to begin in an experiment as new and novel as artistic creation must have been at the dawn of creation; I for one, can only wish them well.

This does not necessarily mean that no alternative is open to the uprooted. I have already mentioned *The Return of the Native* writers and artists from the West Indies who have journeyed to Africa and India in search of their roots. One can only assume that such a journey will help those individuals to reestablish their identities. There have been several cases in which such individuals have returned with only disillusionment, frustration, and apathy; they could not adjust to a culture and society from which they have been removed for two centuries because their present make-up leaves them strangers wherever they go. There are those, however, who have returned with some sense of satisfaction in having revisited their historical past, but their work begins and ends with that "quest." If they serve any function beyond that, it might be said that these works will help future generations to fill *their* historical gap.

It is impossible to escape tradition and the past, even though that tradition and that past may not be entirely one's own. Whether we have been brought up in a society with a small topping of White Europeans as rulers, or among a minority of Blacks within an ongoing culture that is White, we must define ourselves, we must come to understand ourselves within that context, a short and narrow one to be sure since the entire matrix of our heritage is lost in two centuries of silent past.

One of the fundamental elements of the West Indian tradition is colonialism. We are a consumer society, completely dependent upon countries like Britain, the United States, and Canada, and while we are expected to produce the raw materials which are then sent abroad for processing and finishing, some of the psychology of this dependence reflects itself in our entire fabric. An artistic creation *is* a finished product, and it has meaning and relevance within that social milieu, but few West Indians would prefer a local work over something imported. There is something intrinsically good, better, desirable about an import. Is it any wonder then that most West Indian artists live abroad in exile, and is it any wonder then that a large body of West Indian creations continue to be products which are to be consumed abroad with little or no chance of vivifying that milieu from which it is inspired and which it should in turn enrich?

In the case of the expatriate, through time and distance, both language and content suffer. Most West Indian writers in England have at one time or another put their hand to something other than West Indian works which I do not intend to judge here since the critics have already done so. Fortunately for the West Indian writer, there is a large West Indian migration to England, and so his use of West Indian dialect is not completely forgotten, yet, the content of these works "of exile" is clearly different. They are the outcries of a people who are twice uprooted and who have had to come to define themselves in an even newer context, that of a Black immigrant trying to earn a living in the White world, which inculcated all of its values in him and assured him that his place in the Empire would be secure once he had mastered the language, English sports, and a preference for English products. The setting of these works is a grim, grey London, and one of human waste, not only a waste of the immigrants' lives, but the life's work of the artist who should have been creating some body of work which would crystallize just what West Indian culture is, just in what direction it is headed, and just what its peoples are like. One gets extremely nostalgic glimpses of West Indian life from the immigrants in these works. The works deal principally with race and color, but with nothing which could add to that desperately needed core of identity, which to repeat, should be the foremost concern of the artist from the West Indies—an area which cannot afford the luxury of an expatriate Hemingway writing about Spain, Africa, and Cuba.

Recent developments arising from the discontent of students at the University of the West Indies have resulted in the take-over of the Creative Arts Center, a truly impressive structure to house, encourage, and develop dance, drama, music, poetry, painting, sculpture, and the like. And while I do not wish here to discuss student power or student take-over of buildings, it is interesting to note that one of the fundamental reasons for discontent grew from the continued production of European and American plays. Artists from the area were refused production of their works in preference

159

of the imports. The cost of admission was not only beyond the means of the average wage earner in Jamaica, but also clearly supports my earlier statement that the area continues to manifest all of the leftover syndromes of colonialism, understands artistic endeavors purely in terms of the imported, and makes little attempt to encourage works which are rooted in West Indian lore, language, and dialect, all of which are looked down upon as inferior despite the stated aims and purposes of the Creative Arts Center which was clearly meant to engage in a search for a Caribbean identity. There is no question whatsoever in my mind that this continued preference for the imported reflects the tastes and needs of perhaps ten percent of the West Indian population—those who would rather feel amused and entertained by internationally famous "hits" than spend an evening giving audience to works which reach into the bowels of the Caribbean in search of itself.

One of the most vital alternatives seems to be the current-day context of the ongoing social milieu. Most of the problems, questions, situations, and incidents with any kind of dramatic possibilities in the West Indies as well as in the U. S. have at their roots the tensions which result because of a multiracial society. If one does not feel that one should include Whitey in any work written by a Black writer, one is only cutting off one's nose to spoil one's face as an old West Indian saying has it. The late Lorraine Hansberry's play, *Raisin in the Sun*, is a case in point. It deals with a Black family, and it is perhaps one of the first dramatic productions which handles a Black family. Although Whitey was not cast in any role, were not the tensions, the incidents, which made for dramatic possibilities a direct result of this Black family's problems—problems which could only come from the fact that they are uprooted, and that that uprootedness has placed them as a minority in a White society? Granted, the play is a successful one, yet, it has placed upon itself a restriction, a limitation; within this limitation, it manages to come out all right in the end because Miss Hansberry, although she did not find it necessary to introduce Whitey as a character or characters (apart from one minor figure), was nonetheless creating dramatic situations about Blacks which could only be possible within an ongoing society in which Black people are an oppressed minority. Regarded from another perspective, none of the characters in Miss Hansberry's play would be viable outside of a society in which a vast majority are White and the remaining minority of Blacks have had to come to terms with just that imbalance.

Most writers, if asked, "Do you write for yourself? or do you write for some particular audience?" will automatically reject the latter and insist that they write for themselves. There is something intrinsically bad, inferior, about saying that one has some particular audience in mind when one writes. It suggests pandering and mediocrity; it suggests a fettering of the free spirit of the artist. Yet, if we look at West Indian literature, we find that great numbers of West Indian writers have secured for themselves a position which puts them on an equal footing with the finest of English writers. However, witness the readership and the audience which this level, this genre of West Indian writing

161

reaches—perhaps ten percent of the upper crust of West Indian society. The remainder have no opportunity to see themselves, to reflect in any way upon the direction in which their society is headed—what could be more necessary than a reaching out to all levels of any society?

Similarly, the works of Black American writers like Ellison, Wright, and Baldwin were absolutely necessary to their milieu. These forerunners had to insist that a Black man could handle the forms of the day as well as any other man, granted the subject matter and content was taken from Black America. Looked at another way, was it not a need and an attempt to show White America a glimpse of what Black America is like? But what about those large masses of Blacks who so desperately needed to have injected into their lives some essence of the Black experience? The answer is a disappointing one: there was no feedback, just as there was no feedback from those early West Indian writers whose works were read by small numbers of literate and affluent Whites and Blacks.

The need to reach a broader cross section of people in the artist's milieu should be one of his primary concerns, and now that the ground has been broken by those early forerunners, some of the current West Indian and Black American writers are coming to understand this. With this understanding, attempts must be made to reach out to the day-to-day experiences of those neglected masses. A firm grasp and understanding of the incidents of their lives in a singular language with all of its richness and color is called for. These needs suggest that the artist must speak directly to the masses about those issues that are pressing and central to their day-to-day existence.

It was with great satisfaction that I read the introduction to *New Plays from the Black Theater,* an anthology edited by Ed Bullins. The introduction takes the form of an interview in which Mr. Bullins is asked, "How do you feel about all the new Black theatres that are emerging?" And Mr. Bullins replies,

> "I feel good! I feel good! I moved into the theatre for a number of reasons. But I guess it was a natural move because I was writing a number of things. I was busting my head trying to write novels and felt somehow that my people don't read novels. My family doesn't, except for my mother and some of the young kids who are now going to school. But for the great bulk of them, they don't read novels. But when they are in the theatre, I've got them. Or like T.V. You know, my ideas can get to them. So I moved away from prose forms and into the theatre. Black literature has been available to them for years, but it has been circulating in a closed circle . . . the Black Arts circle and the colleges. It hasn't been getting down to the people. But now in the theatre, we can go right into the Black community and have a literature for the people, for the 'people-people,' as Bob Macbeth says . . . for the great masses of Black people. . . ."

Mr. Bullins knows that there is an unreached audience which must be reached, just as I am certain that he knows how they can be reached, and if the form of the novel, or the content of early Black plays have reached only the Black arts circle and the colleges, one has to look somewhere else. If I may repeat, Mr. Gordone's *No Place to be Somebody* has done just that . . . . It has portrayed situations and characters with all of the richness and flavor of language and dialect which presents them with the fullest impact.

It is here that I feel West Indian writers have much to learn, much to come to terms with in trying to reach those masses, whether in the novel or theater form, in an idiom which is their own; that idiom depends heavily upon a use of language and dialect which brings a work to the heart of those long-neglected masses.

In conclusion, since the aims of the West Indian artist are to capture and crystalise the fundamental hopes and aspirations of this emergent area, he must come to terms with his own self-image and identity within his milieu. The Black artist in the United States must do the same in *his* milieu. Having done so, the artist in both cases should find that his total image of himself within his singular context requires of him a presentation, a deliverance of statement, using scenes and situations where his characters speak in their own language and dialect, expressing themselves in *their* terms. An artist can not adequately, honestly, or faithfully make such a presentation without utilizing his own linguistic peculiarities.

NOTES

1. C.L.R. James, "La Divina Pastora" in *Stories from the Caribbean,* ed. Andrew Salkey (London: Elek Books, 1965), pp. 149-150.

SOME SPECULATIONS AS TO THE ABSENCE
OF RACIALISTIC VINDICTIVENESS IN
WEST INDIAN LITERATURE

Austin C. Clarke

The literature I am going to consider in this paper comes from the British West Indies. West Indian literature, or British West Indian, is written mainly in English, with a modern sensibility that tends to render the language relevant to the social and cultural experiences of the people about whom this literature deals. An important aspect of the use of the language by the West Indian writer is the violence contained in the language.

If we considered the geography of the area, and if the geography were consistent with the historical and literary colonization, we would have to talk rather about a Caribbean literature. Caribbean literature, considered as a whole, would have to embrace the writings from Cuba; Haiti; and the French, Dutch, and Portuguese colonies and ex-colonies. One important characteristic of the writings of the Cuban, Haitian, and other European colonies just referred to is the essence of nationalism, or of negritude, or "negrismo." The writing from the British West Indies does not seem to have the factor of negrismo as its outstanding characteristic. It can also be said that British West Indian writing did not achieve the high literary standard of excellence which Cuban literature had won as early as the nineteenth century. There was no strong spirit of nationalism among British West Indian writers at that time. This feeling of negrismo in literature had to wait until the late twentieth century, and it comes mainly from the West Indian writers who emigrated from the West Indies. It might be added that they were forced to utilize nationalism and negrismo in their works because of the pervasive nationalism of the sixties and the seventies. It seems, therefore, that colonization ironically erased from West Indian literature a racial vindictiveness which tended to be an outstanding theme in the literature from Cuba and Haiti, as well as from some of the Spanish-speaking colonies like Brazil. It seems also that some example of excellence or some literary model of good writing existed in those Caribbean colonies where the Spanish influence was strongest.

The racialistic vindictiveness seems on first glance to be correlated to the violence of the colonization of those colonies. In the literature of Cuba in the nineteenth century and later, "the Spaniard is seen to burst into this highly idealized Caribbean Arcadia—cruel, treacherous, lusting for power and wealth."[1] Professor Gabriel Coulthard calls this racialistic vindictiveness in literature, "romantic Indianism." This Indianism in Latin American literature, which is nothing more than negritude as the French-African writers understood the term, had as its characteristic, "an idealization of the Indian and vilification of the Spaniards: Indian heroes and Spanish villains."[2] On the other hand, West Indian writing seems to be an acceptance of the horrors of colonization and a lack of memory of the brutality that went with British West Indian colonization. On the other hand, it really says something very definite about the social structure of West Indian society, in which the presence of the White man, the British colonizer was more or less accepted as a necessary evil. There was, however, no qualitative difference between the colonization of Cuba and Haiti and Brazil and that of the British West Indies. C. L. R. James dispels any thought of paternalistic slavery or colonization in the British West Indies in his brilliant study of slavery, *Black Jacobins.*

The reason for the outstanding quality of Latin American literature in the nineteenth century and the postponement of such high standards in the literature of the British West Indies seems to lie in the absence of literary examples: practically no British slavemaster or British colonialist thought very highly of literature and culture. It is doubtful whether the British in the West Indies were cultured gentlemen at all. It seems, therefore, to be the brand of colonization and the quality of the society of slaves and slave

holders, traders and colonial riff-raff in the British West
Indies that bequeathed a cultural and social life in the islands
distinguished only for its lack of civilized distinction.³ Not
only do the "natural graces" find strangulation in such a
society, but also the literary examples of excellence. Vidia
Naipaul, a West Indian writer from Trinidad saw the lack of
literary examples in the "undesirability" of efficiency in West
Indian society.

> Again and again one comes back to the main,
> degrading fact of the colonial society; it never
> required efficiency, it never required quality, and
> these things because unrequired, became undesir-
> able.⁴

Even if one were to refute the validity of Mr. Naipaul's
statement, in view of his voluntary alienation from his home,
the West Indies, one has still to discuss the reasons why in
1839 a novel like *Cecilia Valdes*, by Cirilo Villaverde, could
achieve an international reputation, and why no such
outstanding literary work came out of the British West Indies
until perhaps *In The Castle Of My Skin* by the Barbadian
writer, George Lamming, in 1953. *A House For Mr. Biswas*,
by V. S. Naipaul, another excellent novel of international
reputation, appeared in 1961.

British West Indian literature must be divided into two
classes: the literature written in the West Indies and the
literature written outside of the West Indies while the writer
is an immigrant of some metropolitan country. The literature
written in the West Indies by West Indians is influenced
(more than expatriate West Indian literature) by what Louis

James calls "a rare and liberating experience of racial sanity;"[5] this "racial sanity," which is in effect a delusion of racial harmony and an unawareness of the presence of Africa as a literary motivation for protest, is what robs the literature of any appreciably significant quality of racialistic vindictiveness. There is not the same intense comprehension of Africa nor any characteristic nationalism in the literature of the West Indies that is written in the West Indies, as is the case with the literature of Latin America. The absence of protest becomes the absence of racialistic vindictiveness, and in turn may be called the absence of nationalism. West Indians have not yet begun to think of themselves as a nation, and this frolicsomeness is also expressed in their literature.

Their literature comes out of a society based more upon an exaction of excellence through sweat than through mental exertion, for masters as well as for slaves. For West Indian creative writers, there was no possibility of a literary imitation of high standards. These writers, with about two exceptions, are Black, of Indian and African ancestry. No Englishman of a higher caste of civilization or culture could withstand the inexpressible horrors of the sugar plantation society, a society propped up by the severest restrictions on the slaves; no Englishman, as a writer, remained in the area long enough to live through the emasculating psychological effects of slavery. There was no model. The West Indian writer, so far as historical antecedents are concerned, came to the area as a slave and as an indentured laborer. Although there is no argument to say that slavery and indenture eradicated the cultural roots or the cultural relevancies of this man from Africa or from India, these writers, either because of their enslavement and their colonization and what these conditions meant to them in a real sense, or because of the peculiar brand of the cultural colonization under which they lived, chose to express their experiences in a literature which omitted the basic quality of their social and cultural predicament. They omitted talking about themselves in phobogenic terms, in terms of themselves as Black men and women living in oppression. "Seen against the various tensions of the area, it is not surprising that many creative Caribbean writers moved away from the West Indies to see their predicament in perspective."[6]

The question of perspective with its implied significance of nationalism, or racialistic vindictiveness, must be viewed against either the West Indian's appreciation of the "various tensions in the area"—that is to say, the heritage of slavery and colonization—or else against his delusion as to its acceptability, or its lack of cultural harshness. This point of acceptability, a kind of Negro American fatalism about life, is the exact opposite of the concept of romantic Indianism that is characteristic of nineteenth-century Cuban literature. What happened in the West Indian's consciousness to rob him of any racialistic vindictiveness against the "villains"? In the novel, *In The Castle Of My Skin*, which deals with the social and cultural dislocations of a group of peasant Black people, in the face of natural and supernatural phenomena, George Lamming has the old woman, Ma, express this so-called Negro fatalism about her lot. She charges her husband, Pa, to see it the same way she does. But Pa and Ma are ex-slaves,

170

and there seems to be a chance for hostility, if not hate, in the kind of lives that they have lived in Barbados. Certainly, one expects them to be vindictive.

> I won't worry my head 'bout the land 'cause 'tis always more trouble than profit, an' in yuh ol' age as you is an' me there be other things we got to think 'bout. Think 'bout the other land, Pa. You may think me stupid and dotish when I tell you these things, but I ain't. An' tell me to besides, Pa, tell me from yuh heart straight to my face why you want to buy this land."[7]

If this resignation to fate is more peculiar to the local West Indian and particularly to the West Indian who is old, and if it can be said, as Louis James suggests, that emigration from the West Indies helps its creative writers to "see their predicament in perspective," it is ironic that Lamming does not introduce this vindictive nationalism in Trumper, the Black Barbadian who had emigrated to the U. S. and has returned to Barbados. But then there is the question, To what extent is the writer's nationalistic consciousness consistent or identical to that of his main character? When Trumper is asked by his mother to relate his experiences in the United States, all he says is,

> There ain't much to say, except that the United States is a place where a man-can-make pots-of-money. Seems a next kind of world. When I tell you I use to have two telephones and three 'lectric fans in a small place o' mine, you can sort o' get my meaning clear.[8]

I do not think that I am doing Mr. Lamming an injustice in singling out these two short extracts from his novel to prove my point. I feel that it is fair to say that nowhere in his novel, *In The Castle Of My Skin*, does one find a glorification of the Black Barbadian peasant at the expense of a villainous characterization of the Englishman. The implication is there, however, but it is only an implication, a subtle one, a sophisticated one; it is one such as a West Indian would make who regards himself more as a Black Englishman than as an African. Lamming names the colonizer "Mr. Slime." He is slimy, that is to say, he is a clever and perhaps a dishonest businessman, but he is nowhere referred to as an essential villain. The other great West Indian novel, *A House For Mr. Biswas*,[9] deals with the economic repercussions of a psychological colonization, and with the attempt of an Indian parent to break through this economic and social suppression by having his son educated at a government secondary school in Trinidad. However, Mr. Biswas did not once see his predicament in terms of the colonialism that engulfed him and his forebears as indentured Indian laborers. Although it was not seen in the same precise mold of a fatalistic mentality, slavery and indenture were never exploited by the writer as the motivations for the delineation of Mr. Biswas' character.

Racialism is not used generally by West Indian writers (those who remain at home and write) as motivation in characterization. However, the possibility of a racialistic vindictiveness does exist for the West Indian writer as it exists for the Black American. "The Black writer is now, of course, able to retaliate; he might speak, as one writer has done, of 'English soldiers smelling of khaki and their race'."[10] But Mr. Naipaul in the same book, *The Middle Passage*, goes on to say that "*to the initiated*" [italics mine], "one whole side of West Indian writing has little to do with literature, and much to do with the race war."[11] The consciousness of racial vindictiveness does reflect itself in the works of West Indians who have left the islands, if only for the sake of being contemporary, or because of the pressures of living in a foreign metropolitan city. Perhaps, this is what Mr. Naipaul means by "the initiated." Louis James contends that the emigrant West Indian writer, rather than seeing his island predicament in perspective—a truer perspective than that which was possible when he resided in a deluded consciousness of racial sanity—finds himself "initiated" into a foreign and perhaps inappropriate nationalism, the intention of which is to introduce, consciously or subconsciously, the factor of negrismo into his work.

It can be said at this point that West Indian literature, written by writers breathing in the "racial sanity" of the islands, is at best an imitation of the literature of English colonizers. Cultural colonization was in essence, the manipulation and the preparation of the West Indian to fit into the bottom of English society, either at home or in the mother country. The success of that preparation, as we see in the literature of the region, killed any spirit of nationalism, any spirit of African consciousness that was more than a comprehension of an idealization of Africa. The schoolmaster, in Lamming's *In The Castle Of My Skin*, replies to a question from one of his students by saying that slavery never existed in Barbados. It is not the historical inaccuracy of the reply that is so tragic: it is the delusion of a whole class of people about their classification as "Black Englishmen." "In the colonial society every man had to be for himself; every man had to grasp whatever dignity and power he was allowed; he had no loyalty to the island and scarcely any to his group."[12] That is why Trumper could ape the speech of Black Americans without at the same time feeling he was imbued with a spirit of their racial vindictiveness. That is why the old woman of *In The Castle Of My Skin* could be unaware of the social significance of Black ownership of the land, and could emphasize instead the financial difficulties of her husband's involvement in the pure monetary aspects of owning the land. There seems to be a general internalizing of the awareness of community, race, and society in most of the characters of West Indian writers. Neither Mr. Biswas, nor Trumper could relate their individual predicament to the larger predicament of Blackness or of racism. This distaste among some West Indian writers for racialistic vindictiveness—although they might be agreeing with Mr. Naipaul who insists that "race cannot be the basis of any serious literature"—is voiced by the Trinidadian novelist, Michael Anthony. Mr. Anthony, who has come from a peasant beginning in Trinidad, and who has lived many years in England during that country's racial problems, can still say,

> I don't want to write any race novels, I just don't want to. It's not my nature. I feel that race novels

usually carry the banner of trying to solve the problem. What they do actually to me is to widen the gulf by creating an awareness of it. [13]

Does Mr. Anthony regard racial awareness in the Black immigrant living in England as being equivalent to racial vindictiveness in his fiction, and is this awareness taken by him as a necessary evil in the same way that Lamming says the Black West Indian accepts the presence of White people in their midst? Or is this racial awareness a kind of fatalism?

The West Indian, like the West Indian writer, was a Black Englishman, if his identity was going to have any meaning in the strict sense of this psychoexistential complex. The psychoexistential complex in the relationship between Blacks and Whites living in a predominantly White culture is a very real phenomenon. As Frantz Fanon uses the term, it defines the meaning of Blackness in the terms of the White majority. Each group defines the other so that in each definition, according to Fanon, lies the possibility of myth. Morality and logic seem to have been absent in such an equation, and what is important here is the power behind the myth, power which gives it both its validity of application and its longevity. The West Indian could then live as if he were in fact an Englishman, a Black Englishman, an English-man of the colonies, so that in his literary expression, so long as he remained in the colonies, he could logically (taking into consideration that he did not regard his life as myth) write about himself and his society as if he was in a transplanted English country. Absent was any attitude of setting the racial record straight; he did not look inward and describe his

175

alienation in his native society, and never once did he question the psychological reasons for that alienation. When he wrote of his West Indian experiences, it was as a man trying desperately to apply an English sensibility about colonialism and English provincialism to Black skin; he produced qualitatively different material from the Black American writer who assumed racialistic vindictiveness against the slave master and his descendants. The wave of riots which visited most of the West Indian islands in the 1930s, which could in other circumstances be given a racialistic explanation in any society but that of the West Indies, were regarded as political and economic rumblings, even though it is very difficult to make this distinction in West Indian society. But the riots, one of "the various tensions of the area," never got substantial literary treatment. The West Indian writer at the time was not concerned, like Michael Anthony, with writing a "race novel." The same is true of the nineteenth-century slave rebellion in Jamaica, the Morant Uprising. Victor Reid, the Jamaican novelist, has written about the Morant Uprising in *New Day*. He has employed the very intricate Jamaican dialect; although this literary flavor does suggest some violence, even if only the violence of the manipulation of the English language by the "natives," still, apart from the obvious virtues of the novel, the treatment of the uprising reads like any other treatment of a battle between two English armies. One does not really smell the Blackness of pride and revenge as one does in the chronicling of the exploits of the great Haitian general, Toussaint L'Ouverture. It can be said that Victor Reid was not so much concerned with making the slave masters into villains as he was obsessed with recording the strengths and the courage of the slaves' assumption of arms.

The best example of this absence of race as a weapon of vindictiveness in West Indian literature is the poem, "A Far Cry From Africa," by Derek Walcott of Trinidad. The poem seems to suggest some awareness of the Mau-Mau uprising in Kenya; the uprising is compared to the gassing of Jews, the cruelty of man, his violence, a "violence of beast on beast" which is regarded as "natural law." Then the poet takes a very startlingly ironic stand when he realizes that he is part of the world of the "gorilla" and of the "superman."

> I who am poisoned with the blood of both,
> Where shall I turn, divided to the vein?
> I who have cursed
> The drunken officer of British rule, how choose
> Between this Africa and the English tongue I love?
> Betray them both, or give back what they give?
> How can I face such slaughter and be cool?
> How can I turn from Africa and live? [14]

This poem was published in 1962. It might have been written in 1960, but that is not important. What is important is that during the fifties and sixties in America, Black people were beginning to identify with Africa in music, in literature, and in social and cultural matters. Malcolm X had already said he "despised the White traces of blood in his veins." Marcus Garvey, fifty years before, had eulogized Africa to such an extent that he wrapped thousands of Black people throughout the world in a cultural Black nationalism; still, one finds some cultural and ancestral conflict in this poet.

Nationalism in literature, or racial vindictiveness, involves the colonial or ex-colonial writer's deliberate attempt to turn the tables on previous writers—almost all of whom were certainly White—who explained both the colonial and colonial society and who presumed to portray the full dimension of the Black or colonial experience from the perspective of the psychoexistential relationship equation. It was an attempt to complete the colonization of the West Indians by assuming that in the master-slave relationship lay the possibility of the master's full comprehension and complete knowledge of Blackness and of Black people in a literary expression that was not based on myth. Decolonization means reevaluation. Reevaluation means repudiation. Repudiation of colonization must include a rejection of all myths, even a rejection of literary standards of the colonization period. None of these phenomena occurred in the British West Indies to any significant extent. The West Indian writer living at home chose not to exploit them. Since the West Indian, as a citizen and a writer, could delude himself into believing that he was living in a society free of racialistic tensions, that he was indeed a free man (if the title of Black Englishman was reprehensible to him!), then he could live with the myth of a new psychoexistential equation which proposed that Black was equal to, if not superior to, White. In fact it can be said that he refused to choose: "...how choose/Between this Africa and the English tongue I love?" It is not language that Walcott is talking about here.

It is rather language as it is defined in terms of an English colonial sensibility. If one is obsessed by this English colonial sensibility, then not even one's language can be violent. One becomes convinced of the possibility of betrayal based upon a split personality "poisoned with the blood of both." The West Indian writer, like the West Indian citizen, "does not feel the need to try to understand an Englishman, since all relationships begin with an assumption of previous knowledge, *a knowledge acquired in the absence of the people known*" [italics added]. "This relationship with the English is only another aspect of the West Indian's relation to the *idea* of England."[15] This criticism, which is applied primarily to the West Indian away from home, is equally applicable to the West Indian writer at home faced with the choice of whether or not to relate his literary material to his colonial environment.

One, therefore, finds that instead of an awareness of nationalism in literature, there is a certain violence in the language of the literature. The violence I am talking about has nothing to do with the blood and the bullet and the raped television set in the Black American ghettoes. It has rather to do with the possibility, perhaps also the desirability, of those bullets and blood and television sets being used to manipulate and mangle the English language into something as brutal and vicariously nationalistic as West Indian language. Leopold Senghor was critized for dressing negritudinous literary expressions in the French colonialist language. Frantz Fanon, the Martinican psychiatrist, insists that it is schizophrenic to use the colonizer's language to write about

.

179

the liberation of the colonized. It seems that the West Indian writer, a man from a society ostensibly free of the worst pathologies of racialism, a man from a society into which Black nationalism had to be imported from American Blacks (like most other attitudes and fashions and styles—styles of living included), could do nothing more than couch his literary expression in the pathology of self-identity and crisis, personal crisis, and the concept *machismo* (related to the conquest of woman) within the social framework of the particular island in which he lived. He could do no more than define his relation to the land and to the women around him who outnumber him. He could do nothing more than question himself about his identity within a Caribbean island framework, and then in turn ask himself to what extent was he alienated within his own society. "This may be the dilemma of the West Indian writer abroad: that he hungers for nourishment from a soil which he (as an ordinary citizen) could not at present endure."[16] The West Indian writer's conception of soil, while he is at home, has nothing to do with the symbolic meaning of soil. It does not even embrace his longing for the possession of his soil which he takes for granted. The exposure of his delusion about owning the soil is really what robs his work of the vitality which it could otherwise have. "This vitality can only be achieved when the colonial castration of the West Indian sensibility has been healed."[17] He ignored the wound while he was at home; at least he did not know it existed then: it is doubtful that emigration would prove to be a solution. George Lamming has said, in *The Pleasures of Exile*, that West Indians lack any real knowledge of the Englishmen living among them. Perhaps what he is saying is that we do not understand Whiteness, if Whiteness can be defined monolithically as symbolic of oppression. The West Indian accepts, he went on to say, the White presence as a necessary evil, as part of the landscape. There is something more than psychological security intended here for the West Indian is in the political majority. There is also an absence of racialism in the attitude: no threat to life or limb. But there certainly is a threat to our real knowledge of ourselves, our meaning to ourselves. We see no significant emphasis on nationalism or racial vindictiveness in the works of writers who live at home or who write about home as a romanticization of fact based upon memory and boyhood reflection, a memory idealized perhaps through the distance and safety of departure from the islands. We see no appreciable conscious Africanization of literary themes. The West Indian writer has avoided such Africanization; he "has so far avoided the American Negro type of protest writing, but his aims have been equally propagandist: to win acceptance for his group."[18] This is not wholly true for the West Indian writer living abroad.

Michael Anthony, in his novel *The Games Were Coming*, is more concerned about the *machismo* of his hero Leon—the pressures upon him to win a cycle race, to keep his woman, and to maintain the hero-worship that goes with excellence in sports—than he is concerned with the social-psychological fabric on which the cycle race takes place. It takes place during Carnival in Trinidad, and Carnival in Trinidad can be said to be, among other things, an economic exploitation by the tourist industry and by the merchants of the island, during which the poor of Trinidad are expected to deplete the inexhaustible piled-up shelves in the stores. In *A Man From The People*, by Lionel Hutchinson of Barbados, micro-national politics on the island, complete with bribes, free-rum campaigning, and sexual conquests by the candidates, are discussed by the author of this first West Indian political novel; however, nowhere in the book does Mr. Hutchinson relate the political and social dreams of the islanders—for that's what they are—to the condition of the colonized mentality obsessed with dispossessing the colonizers. In fact, Mr. Hutchinson does not see the White segment of the population, which is practically invisible in the book, as any cause for this political battle of crabs; certainly, it is a battle of crabs, planned many years before in history, in a precise strategy that came out of the psycho-existential equation.

The calypsonian, "The Mighty Sparrow," one of the best poets to have come out of the West Indies, can sing of the role which education plays in a developing society (much the same way that Mr. Biswas understood the essential meaning of education for his son), "to earn, to earn, you got to learn," but he failed to relate this belated availability of free education in the young independent nation to any sin of racial omission on the part of the colonizers, who certainly have kept the people uneducated and undereducated. In another calypso about education, Sparrow talks about the inappropriate and irrelevant school text books that most West Indians used. While he vividly points to these damaging factors in education, he dismisses this mis-education itself as "stupidness." It certainly is not stupidness: the minds of thousands of colonial and ex-colonial Black children have already been warped. Hatred and hostility and what Naipaul calls "the English smelling of khaki"—that kind of racialistic vindictiveness is absent from the literature, in the main. The fete in the language of the calypso and the fete in the language of the writer are too intoxicating for us to grasp the basic sensibility, and that is a kind of colonial sensibility that is certainly not stupidness.

"The involvement of the Negro with the White world," says Naipaul,

> is one of the limitations of West Indian writing, as it is the destruction of American Negro writing. The American Negro's subject is his blackness. This cannot be the basis of any serious literature, and it has happened again and again that once the American Negro has made his statement, his profitable protest, he has nothing to say.[19]

Mr. Naipaul's dogmatism is more extreme than the hesitations of Michael Anthony for not wanting to write what he called, a "race novel." Race seems to be a despicable term to West Indians, but West Indians generally have ignored race in their daily lives, in their "involvement with the White world." They have spent a lot of time writing about "lumps of earth; unrefined, perhaps, but good, warm, fertile earth."[20] Involvement, on the one hand, suggests not only a multiracial society, but also one half of the psychoexistential equation; the fertility of soil suggests that there is an inward

183

search going on at the same time as the involvement with the White world. Involvement and fertility, if they are simultaneous, may bring about a kind of literary schizophrenia, a kind of "poisoning with the blood of both" since the blood has divided West Indian consciousness of nationalism, cultural nationalism, to the very vein, as the poet says. This fertility of the soil, which Lamming maintains is the gift of West Indian literature to the Old World, is a fertility of language only. Even though Samuel Selvon, the distinguished Trinidadian novelist, can confess that "cane is bitter" (sugar cane, not the biblical character) which may imply a certain native sensibility about the land and about the psychological implications of Indians and African-West Indians being tied to the sugar cane fields, still the bitterness very seldom is a bitterness of vilification or of racialistic vindictiveness.

West Indian literature which contains a stronger aspect of nationalism and White vilification comes from those West Indians who do not live at home. It is questionable, as Louis James maintains in his introduction to *The Islands In Between*, whether these exiled West Indian writers can see their "predicament in perspective." Of course, Mr. James did not tell us whether he was referring to their "predicament" as West Indians in the West Indies, or in exile, or whether he was talking about their "predicament" as West Indians who refuse, generally, like the immigrant West Indians in New York City, to regard themselves as Black and be involved in the problems of Black people in that part of the world. Whether or not the West Indian can see his "predicament" at all, he is at the same time an exile, an escapist, an immigrant, and he has become imbued (to varying degrees) with the respective radicalism or Black nationalism of the time and place of his sojourn. It is, therefore, from these West Indians living in Canada, Britain, France, and the United States that the literature takes on, in varying degrees of their attachment to the Black consciousness of their new locations, the quality of racialistic vindictiveness.

This is not to say that even as far away as the West Indies is from the metropolitan centers of radicalism, one does not find a socially conscious West Indian. It is rather that living abroad, as Louis James suggested, this man is in a position to see his "predicament" in some perspective. The important point about this new awareness of his predicament, and his staunch or vicarious attachment to Black nationalism, is that basically, it is a political and cultural phenomenon that is external and may well be superficial, since it did not form a significant part of his colonial sensibility. If this is what Naipaul means by the limitation of West Indian writing caused by the writer's involvement in the White world, and if this is the reason why "blackness cannot be the basis of any serious literature," then the point is well taken. But if he means that the West Indian writer, whose Blackness or consciousness is rubbed off on him during his sojourn abroad, writes out of this borrowed Black consciousness and cannot write serious literature, then I think that Mr. Naipaul's dogmatism fails to take into consideration the possibility of this new perspective being used by the West Indian writer to comment, artistically in a literary way, on the very serious social significance of Black-White relations.

185

Perhaps the question really lies on the matter of treatment of Blackness by the West Indian writer abroad, and not so much on the content in his book of that Blackness. Blackness and Whiteness as content in literature are one and the same thing: *race*. If Blackness, or race, is, *ipso facto*, not a very serious content for high literature, then writers like William Faulkner and Mark Twain, two White American writers of great reputation, would have to be reevaluated, because Whiteness (and Blackness) is all that they talked about in their works. So, it has to be the treatment of the racialistic vindictiveness or nonvindictiveness in literature that Mr. Naipaul is talking about. This vindictiveness in any literature seems to be based upon the immediacy of racialism in the society, an immediacy which governs each mental vibration, each aspect of each breath of a colonial experience, and which in turn, impinges itself upon the consciousness of the writer. I do not think that the *Confessions of Nat Turner* may be dismissed as serious literature merely because it deals with Blackness and with Whiteness, that is to say, because it is a race novel. It seems also that the novel, *dem*, by William Melvin Kelly, which deals with Blackness, is also a very serious piece of literature.

This Blackness in awareness, a new perspective of the West Indian's predicament in the Old World, whether it is natural, or merely a condition of his predicament, is a major feature of the novels written by those who escaped the West Indies. One exception is, of course, V. S. Naipaul, who does not write in an obviously vindictive style as if he were concerned with setting any record straight. Mr. Naipaul has assumed a curious brand of cultural assimilation within the pure English culture. Michael Anthony is another exception, and his reasons, though surprising for a creative person, are understandable. It is not in his nature to write about race. The other West Indian novelists living abroad have written works in which there is the treatment of Blackness in a racialistically vindictive way. Samuel Selvon has done it, although at the same time he was more concerned with the literary style of humor and satire. But the vilification is there, if only implied. Andrew Salkey, Jan Carew, and George Lamming have become "Blacker," as the saying goes, in their works.

The most important example of nationalism or racialistic vindictiveness in West Indian literature comes from the poet Edward Brathwaite. Mr. Brathwaite who came out of the Barbadian brand of colonial sensibility studied in Britain, taught and lived in Africa, and then returned to the West Indies, but paid frequent visits to such places in America as Harlem. He can say, in all literary seriousness:

> Build now
> the new
> villages, you
> must mix spittle
> with dirt, dung
> to saliva and
> sweat: round
> mud walls will rise
> in the dawn.[21]

There is no ambivalence in Mr. Brathwaite's literature; even though he is a West Indian like Derek Walcott—that is he was subjected to the same twin-consciousness of African Blackness and English colonialism—there is no room in his consciousness for singing about "I who am poisoned with the blood of both where shall I turn, divided to the vein?" Mr. Brathwaite understands the background from which Mr. Walcott comes, but he understands the injustice in that background, so it is racially logical for him to say in the same collection of poems, *The Rights of Passage*:

> Cut the cake—
> walkin', man; bus'
> the crinoline off the white woman,
>
> man; be the black buttin' ram
> that she makes you
> an' let's get to hell out'a Pharoah's land![22]

The violence is not only in the language: it is also psychological, and it is real. It is something suggesting the radicalism of the Muslims in America. Certainly the line "let's get to hell out'a Pharoah's land!" suggests that kind of nationalism and racialistic pride. This new Black awareness in West Indian literature written by expatriate West Indians, this new racialistic vindictiveness, is here suggested as a wholesome indication that the "colonial sensibility" that George Lamming talked about in *The Pleasure of Exile* is perhaps the first stage of the West Indian writer's ability to see his "predicament in a new perspective." It may be an external factor which he applies to his literary expression. But in the context of his new psychoexistentialism, it is a realistic expression. There seems to be nothing else he can do.

So what to do, man?
Ban the Bomb? Bomb
the place down?

Boycott the girls? [by which the poet means *white* girls!]
Put a ban on all
Marriages? Call
You'self X

wear a beard
and a turban
washing your tur-
bulent sex

about six
times a day:
going Muslim?
Black as God

Brown is good
white as sin?
An' doan forget Jimmy Baldwin
an' Martin Luther King. . . [23]

The West Indian writer abroad is becoming imbued with the concept of "Black aesthetics" that seems to pervade the literature of contemporary Black Americans. One does not have to become involved in an argument about the meaning of literature, or whether race or Blackness is a serious enough factor on which to base high art, in order to see that what the

West Indian writer is writing about today is the meaning of Blackness and Whiteness in a postcolonial mental condition, and about the way in which this defines him as a man. Not only are the fiction writers and the poets becoming more attuned to nationalism in literature, but the West Indian essayists and historians and sociologists, too, are trying to make the record more relevant, if not more true to the West Indian condition of life, past and present. Sociologist Orlando Patterson has done much work in this field,[24] so has Raymond Smith. Edward Brathwaite is also a historian, and his recent book about the presence of Africa in the West Indies, together with the other original studies of West Indian writers of nonfiction, have done much to correct the myth of the colonial who served as the interpreter of the West Indies. This correction will assume some repudiation of the White point of view. It may involve, and imply, some vilification. It could be racialistically vindictive in the positive way in which I suggested that vindictiveness of this kind is the essential first step in understanding the West Indian predicament. His predicament, which is diversely psychological, includes his delusion of having lived in a multicolor, multiracial society without understanding the historical reasons for that kind of society; his delusion about his own freedom, at home and in his heart; and the juxtaposition of his emigration from the island with the new reality of being Black in a White society in which he is a stranger. These are social factors which bring out nationalism if not anger in most men. If these factors constitute the West Indian's experiences, then as a writer he is bound to deal with them.

The reasons which partially brought about the great popularity of West Indian literature in Britain and throughout the world were based on the *exotic equality* of the language and the treatment of the works: what Lamming calls "the good, warm, fertile soil." West Indian literature, written by West Indians both living at home and abroad, brought to the English language and literature a certain freshness, a certain style, a certain "tribalization" as Marshall McLuhan would say. However, this exotic nature in the works gradually went out of style because the West Indian writer was also a man, a citizen; his racialistic awareness became more imbued with the ethic of Black awareness which was basically foreign to his sensibilities and which encroached upon them through closeness to a society that was no longer only colonialist, but actually oppressive. If the racialistically vindictive aspect in Black literature can be said to come out of the crushing social experiences in the lives of these writers, and if it is their reflection of this unnatural social dynamic (if LeRoi Jones and Richard Wright have to be vindictive, if they have to be Black in a total sense in order to maintain sanity even when they are creating their literature), then in a society which is less immediately oppressive—as the West Indian society is or is deluded into thinking so of itself—the literature of the West Indian writer at home will reflect both the delusion of colonial cultural assimilation and also express itself in literal styles that are less racialistically vindictive. Since the presence of the White man and the symbolic representation of the White world did not present so harshly in a physical sense the racialism of the

United States, and since this White presence, whether individually or collectively, could be taken for granted—as George Lamming suggests, "an unavoidable evil"—then to write about this psychoexistential relationship between Whites and Blacks in a West Indian context will be to write about an experience which did not exploit race in the same sense that some Black American writers use Blackness as the literary basis of their work.

The basic quality of West Indian writing in its natural setting is, therefore, not concerned either with the ejection or even the rejection of the White presence. There is no Cuban prototype of romantic Indianism. Even the great calypsonian, "The Mighty Sparrow," living in a country which historically is the only one in recent times to have a Black Power revolt, could be unaware of the Black American castigation of Martin Luther King as some kind of "Uncle Tom," and could in turn, glorify him in a calypso. It is a testament to Sparrow's political naiveté that in another calypso, he praised President John Kennedy for making the Russian ships turn back from aiding Cuba in that country's crisis.

In the case of the literature written by the West Indian living in a metropolitan country, his presence upon that White landscape of racialistic sensibilities, perhaps the fact that he might not breathe his next breath, is directly related to how he is seen by the host society, the Whites, and this experience must provide him with an attitude which one would expect to be less delusory. It might even make him "change his name to X." Certainly, he would not be "divided to the vein." His sense of a mental and spiritual nationalism would tend under the circumstances of his experiences to make him not only vindictive in his thoughts, but perhaps even physically vindictive, because he understands now what it is to

> "sweat
> in this tin trunk'd house
>
> that we rent from the rat
> to share with the mouse. . ." [25]

NOTES

1. G. R. Coulthard, *Race and Colour in Caribbean Literature* (London: Oxford Univ. Press, 1962), p. 7.

2. Ibid, p. 7.

3. James Anthony Froude, *The English in the West Indies* (1887), passim.

4. V. S. Naipaul, *The Middle Passage* (London: Deutsch, 1962), p. 58.

5. Louis James, ed., *The Islands In Between* (London: Oxford Univ. Press, 1968), p. 4.

6. Ibid., p. 4.

7. George Lamming, *In The Castle Of My Skin* (London: Michael Joseph, 1953), p. 87.

8. Ibid., p. 282.

9. I regard both *In The Castle Of My Skin* and *A House For Mr. Biswas* as West Indian novels in the sense that the mental sensibilities and the cultural reference point of each author were essentially West Indian, even though both authors wrote their

novels while living in Britain. The separation from the West Indies, although definite and physical at that point, was not as distinctly cultural as it later became.

10. V. S. Naipaul, *The Middle Passage*, p. 68.

11. Ibid., p. 68.

12. Ibid., p. 72.

13. C. L. R. James and Michael Anthony, *Discovering Literature in Trinidad: Two Experiences, The Journal of Commonwealth Literature*, No. 7 (July 1969): 86.

14. Derek Walcott, *In a Green Night* (London: Jonathan Cape, 1963), p. 18.

15. George Lamming, *The Pleasures of Exile* (London: Michael Joseph, 1960), p. 25.

16. George Lamming, *The Pleasures of Exile*, p. 50.

17. Ibid., p. 49.

18. V. S. Naipaul, *The Middle Passage*, p. 69.

19. V. S. Naipaul, *The Middle Passage*, p. 69.

20. George Lamming, *The Pleasures of Exile*, p. 46.

21. Edward Brathwaite, *The Rights of Passage* (London: Oxford Univ. Press, 1967), p. 4.

22. Ibid., p. 20.

23. Ibid., p. 55.

24. *The Sociology of Slavery* by Patterson; Raymond Smith's article "People and Change" [New World magazine, Guyana Independence Issue (1966)]; and Brathwaite's new book, together with *British Historians in the West Indies* by Eric Smith, are attempts by West Indian writers to set the record straight, though not to vilify the English, although this may be synonymous.

25. Edward Brathwaite, *The Rights of Passage*, p. 39.

SOME NOTES ON BRAZIL'S BLACK THEATRE

Frederic M. Litto

The following paper attempts to give an account of one aspect of the theatrical scene in Brazil: its Blackness, that is, how Black people have fared and are faring in the art as subjects and participants. A major obstacle before me, I suspect, is the fact that you and I do not have a common context in which to place and evaluate my remarks. While Africa not very long ago lost the appellation "The Dark Continent," I fear that South America has now picked it up. Unless we understand how the Brazilian reality differs from the African and Afro-American realities, we will not understand why cultural patterns there have the configurations

195

Frederic M. Litto

they do. I strongly believe that it is essential for us to understand that reality, for it may have some serious lessons for us as Americans and as students of the African dispersion.

Let us, at the outset, dispel any notions we may have about Brazil's being a racial democracy, the sort of racial paradise mentioned in touristic guides and grade school texts. In point of fact, Brazil's racial situation lies about midway between the harmonious conditions in most of the Black-governed new nations of Africa and the awesome racial struggle presently going on in the United States. Almost 40 percent of Brazil's nearly one hundred million inhabitants are Black, putting Brazil into a position to rival Nigeria for having the largest Black population in the world. The numerical extent of this Black population is yet another of the several reasons why many Brazilians take umbrage when they are called Latin Americans.[1] A "Latin" country would be essentially Caucasian, and Brazil is clearly not that. The census of 1960 determined that Brazil's racial make-up was 60 percent Caucasian, 26 percent Mulatto, 11 percent Negro, 2 percent Amerindian, and 1 percent Asian.[2]

Just as Blacks in North America helped to build our civilization, Blacks in Brazil were the physical and mental forces instrumental in the development of the Portuguese overseas empire. Brazil was discovered by the pioneering Portuguese navigator Pedro Alvares Cabral in 1500, and in 1538 the first African slaves arrived, marking the establishment of a forced-labor economy that lasted over three hundred years. In the seventeenth and eighteenth centuries, more than three million Black slaves entered Brazil, but

196

slavery in the Portuguese-language world differed from North American slavery in several important ways, the most significant one being the many opportunities slaves had for manumission.[3] Thus, by 1798 there were 406,000 free Negroes in Brazil, and by the time of the abolition of slavery in 1888 there were three times as many freed men as slaves. In what was probably a well intentioned effort to eradicate a shameful part of history, the government destroyed almost all the documents and physical evidence of slavery, an act now rued by contemporary historians and called "the perfect racial crime" by certain modern Brazilian intellectuals. But the specter of slave days lingers on. Why else was it necessary for Brazil to pass the "Afonso Arinos" Law of 1950 which punishes racial discrimination? Why does the percentage of Blacks in Brazilian schools today total only about 1 percent? Why, when one reads the leading Brazilian newspapers and magazines, does one customarily find pictures of Negroes only in articles on football and the samba schools, and only rarely in articles on the military-government-industry-high society complex?

The usual explanation is that instead of racial prejudice, Brazil has class prejudice. Charles Wagley, the Columbia University anthropologist, has observed that "Brazil has avoided developing a caste society such as that of the United States, where the strict line between the Negro and the white has been such a costly drain upon the nation and the individual."[4] Wagley's studies on Brazil have shown that other factors are more important than race to the average Brazilian; that wealth, occupation, education, family

197

connections, and physical beauty are primary considerations before and beyond race; and that social position in the society is determined by them, with a consequent freedom for upward movement for those who are able to manipulate these factors to their own individual advantages. Brazilians, in fact, have a saying: "A rich Negro is a white man and a poor white is a Negro."[5] More recent studies, however, have shown that "in a very complex societal mechanism, race consciousness supports class distinctions, and *vice versa*."[6]

Brazilians are "acutely conscious" of physical race, not so much for discrimination, as is the case in other countries, but as "a system by which individuals are described . . . a way of disguising a person's probable social rank . . . [and] a mechanism by which 'people of colour' can avoid the stigma of being classed as Negroes."[7] I have compiled from various sources, including Wagley, a list of *some* of the different racial classifications or types that Brazilians refer to in daily conversations.[8] Note that most of the definitions of these subtle distinctions depend principally upon intensity of skin pigmentation and quality of hair.

> *branco—* white, well made mouth, fine lips and nose, "good" (i.e., straight) hair
> *prêto—* very black, with coarse or curly hair, thick lips, and broad nose
> *mulato—* not as dark as *prêto*, with "bad" hair, or slightly curled hair
> *tapuia—* having the physical features of the Amerindian
> *pardo—* an official term "to include people of various racial mixtures who are not clearly Negroid, Amerindian, or Caucasoid"

mestiço— same as *pardo*
cabo verde— black, but with "good" hair
moreno claro— literally, light brunette
moreno alvo— lighter than *moreno claro*
moreno escuro— literally, dark brunette
moreno côr de canela— literally, cinammon-colored
amarelo— "has no blood"; very pale and with any
    sort of hair
gazo— very white, with blue eyes; "too white"
sarará— "ant" colored, with "bad" hair
caboclo— moreno with "good" hair; "copper-
    colored"; much like *cabo verde*; also Indian
    and Caucasian mixture.
mameluco— mixture of Indian and Caucasian
    features
curiboca or *cariboca—* mixture of Indian and
    Caucasian features
cafuzo— mixture of Indian and Negroid features
preto cafuzo— mixture of Indian and Negroid
    features
mulato crioulo—
cabra— lighter-colored skin, not shiny
chulo— tobacco-colored skin, with tightly curled
    hair
creolo— tobacco-colored skin, with wavy hair

Curiously enough, the word *negro* (black) in Brazil is a derogatory term, whereas *prêto* (Black) is not. When Wagley carried out his research in 1950-1951 in the northeast, where the greatest concentration of Black people in the country exists, he found that the term *negro* is seldom heard and then only in anger. "The label *'negro ruim'* (bad Negro) is a powerful insult."[9] The sociological literature, in fact, clearly

199

documents the fact that there are other fascinating contradictions among Brazilians regarding matters of race. On the one hand most Brazilian women prefer to give birth to light-colored children; such women are said to have a *barriga limpa* (clean stomach), and a woman who gives birth to a child darker than herself is said to have a "dirty" stomach. [10] This is an example of the "morbid anxiety for the acquisition of the status of 'whiteness'" that Brazilian sociologists are now examining intensively. [11] On the other hand, people of mixed ancestry in Brazil can be considered extremely attractive; for example, the *morena* (Caucasian features with darker skin) is "the ideal feminine beauty," and the *mulata* has been celebrated in verse and song, and remembered in men's last wills and testaments for centuries in Brazil. [12] Likewise, the Brazilians show their pride in racial mixtures by telling the following story: One man says to another, "What animal is the strongest you know?" The answer: "The burro! And do you know why? Because the burro is a mixture. Now tell me, who is the strongest person you know?" The answer: "The Brazilian! And why? Because he is a mixture, just like the burro!" [13]

The Africans brought as slaves to the New World carried with them, as part of their "cultural baggage," dramatic dances and ceremonies. A theater without written texts, passed on orally, anonymous, directly related to the world view of the performers and the spectators—this was a vital, living art. The vestiges of it can still be found in certain areas of Brazil today, particularly the northeast, and Africanists who search in vain within Africa for explanations of certain historical problems of culture may well find answers in the field even today in Brazil.[14] We know, for example, that slaves in the sixteenth century performed dance-dramas, like the *congada* or the *congo*, the *quicumbre*, the *taieiras*, and the *quilombos*, all of African origin; the famous *bumba-meu-boi*, whose earliest origins are still unclear, shows definite African influences.[15] The slaves performed skits of their own composition in the season between Christmas and Epiphany. Understandably enough, they were often presented much like Portuguese *autos* of the sixteenth century. In time, though, a new class of Brazilians arose who were to make an important contribution to the theater. These were the mulattoes, who, already of low class, yet possibly free from servitude because they were often the illegitimate offspring of the aristocrats, easily entered the shamefully-viewed acting profession. Though they usually played only in the secondary and base roles written for them, some were able to surmount enormous social difficulties and leave their marks in Brazilian theatrical history. We remember today the names of Father Ventura, the hunchbacked mulatto who built the first permanent theater in Rio de Janeiro in 1767; Chica da Silva, the Negro woman, celebrated in other chapters of Brazilian history, who between 1753 and 1771 operated a private theater near Diamantina in Minas Gerais State; and the former slave Vitoriano, remembered for his interpretation in 1790 of *Tamerlão na Persia* (Tamerlaine in Persia) in Cuiabá in Mato Grosso State.

It is not generally known that many slaves freed in Brazil chose to return to Africa. Some of these returnees made a considerable impact on their home communities by introducing ideas which were an amalgam of European and New World ways. Perhaps the most notable effect was the Brazilian "school" of architecture that held sway in Yorubaland. Another manifestation was the unusual group called the Brazilian Dramatic Company. Theater life in Lagos in the late nineteenth century was characterized by the "concert," a theatrical event promoted for the normal love of expression through dance, song, and ritual found around the world, but also because of the desire on the part of the small Lagos elite to demonstrate an interest in music and theatre to the extent that these were symbols of European status and culture. [16] This elite included a "Brazilian Community," which increased in number after emancipation in Brazil. On 23 May 1882, in honor of Queen Victoria's birthday, a "Brazilian Dramatic Company, under the patronage of the German Consul, performed a 'grand theatre'!" The record shows that the stage was "tastefully decorated," and that the performance consisted of "humorous, dramatic and other pieces, songs and performances on the violin and the guitar." [17] The event was so successful that repeat performances were requested. Some of the members of this Black dramatic society, with Brazilian-acquired names like da Costa, Campos, Barboza, and Silva, eventually became leaders in Lagos concert circles. Unfortunately, the "concert" movement did not last more than a few decades, for it lacked "strong and independent roots in the Nigerian soil."

In the realm of playwrighting, early Brazilian Blacks, or really mulattoes, left their traces, unconsciously carrying on the tradition begun by Afonso Álvares, the seventeenth-century Portuguese mulatto who was the first author of African descent to write literary works in a European language.[18] Notable among these Black Brazilians was Machado de Assis, renowned prose writer, founder of the Brazilian Academy of Letters, and sometime playwright. Machado, like many other Black Brazilian authors of the nineteenth century, enjoyed a social status that no North American writer of African descent then ever dreamed of having.[19] But it must be said that like Black writers everywhere at that time, the Brazilians had to adhere to European norms of style and form, for "Africanisms were not recognized as such, but [were] regarded as mistakes and expunged."[20]

This meant that Blacks were consistently represented in drama in ridiculous, stereotyped ways. "Black-boy" parts were included in nineteenth-century plays as picturesque caricatures. The great masterpieces of Brazilian romanticism and comedy of social manners, the plays of José de Alencar, Martins Pena, Artur Azevedo, and others, all treat the Black character in a fashion whose only virtue was its consistency.

The Brazilian stage remained as described until 1944, when a new face appeared on the scene, that of Abdias do Nascimento, a Negro born in 1914 in the city of Franca in the western part of São Paulo State. The son of a shoemaker and a seamstress, Nascimento delivered groceries while going to school, became a rural schoolteacher, and in 1930 joined the Brazilian Army. He subsequently took a bachelor's degree in economic sciences at the University of Rio de Janeiro, and in the early 1940s he worked variously as a newspaper reporter, an accountant, and a bank manager, and he traveled extensively through the rest of South America.[21] After attending a meeting at the University of San Marcos in Lima, Peru, in 1941, Nascimento went to the Municipal Theater to see Eugene O'Neill's *The Emperor Jones*. Though moved by the play and the performance in general, he felt that the White actor playing Jones in blackface was simply not up to the emotional strength required by the part. He asked himself: Wasn't a Negro actor available for the role?[22] He then tried to recall if he had ever seen a play in Brazil in which the leading role had been represented by a Black. The answer, of course, was negative, and it forced him to consider whether or not Brazil was really a racial democracy. Nascimento quickly recognized that most plays on the Brazilian stage were either by foreign authors, or by Brazilians following European models in theme and form. And this more than twenty years after São Paulo's Semana de Arte Moderna (1922), the signal event in Brazilian culture marking the breaking away from European literary and artistic contexts and the pursuit of cultural autonomy. The theater, as usual, was well behind its sister arts.

It took some time for his ideas to fall into place, but by the end of 1944, Nascimento was ready. With the help of Black and White intellectuals and artists, he founded the Teatro Experimental do Negro [T.E.N.], an organization "that would open the role of protagonist to the Negro, enable him to rise from his status as a secondary or folkloric character to become the *subject* and the hero of the plays in which he appeared."[23] At first Nascimento did not see the organization's creation arising from the need for vindication or protest; rather it was "a defense of the cultural reality of Brazil." Everything was against him in his effort, and theater is a medium that requires the cooperation of many people. The press attacked him by saying that such a theater was not necessary because theater doors were open to Blacks everywhere. The various agencies of government refused to cooperate at first because government policy had it that Blacks did not exist as a separate entity in Brazilian life—everyone in Brazil was a Brazilian and that was that. There was a further obstacle in that the first persons to turn out for T.E.N. were government workers, typists, laborers, and domestics. Some had to be taught to read first, and so Nascimento did that. The group's first effort was a collaboration with a student theater on a play called *Palmares*, probably about the famous slave revolt in the Northeast in the seventeenth century, and a favorite subject of freedom-loving Brazilians.[24] Then Nascimento found that his theater lacked plays which were in accord with his thinking. He rejected most retrospective national dramatic literature because of its stereotyping, of course, and so turned outside Brazil. Eugene O'Neill gave Nascimento special permission to perform all his plays without royalty payments, so the first three plays done by T.E.N. were *The Emperor Jones*, given a splashy single performance in the Teatro Municipal of Rio on 8 May 1945; *All God's Chillun Got Wings*, performed in 1946 at the Teatro Fenix in Rio; and *The Dreamy Kid*. Finally, in 1947 the first play written especially for the company appeared: *O Filho Pródigo* (The Prodigal Son) by Lúcio Cardoso, performed on 5 December at the Teatro Ginástico in Rio. Then came a spate of Black-oriented plays: *Aruanda* (the mythical home of the gods in African religion) by Joaquim Ribeiro (Teatro Ginástico, 23 December 1948); *Filhos de Santo* (literally, Sons of the Saint; officers in the *candomblé* ceremonies) by José de Morais Pinho (Teatro Regina, Rio, 27 March 1949); *Rapsódia Negra* (Negro Rapsody), a ballet-drama by Nascimento (1952), and *Sortilégio*, a drama by Nascimento (Teatro Municipal, Rio, 21 August 1957, and later in São Paulo). It appears that T.E.N. also prepared for production Garcia Lorca's *Amor de don Penlimplín con Belisa en su Jardin*, (The Love of Don Penlimplin with Belisa in her Garden),[25] Camus' *Caligula*, Gheon's *The Road of the Cross*, and Langston Hughes's *Mulatto*, but details are lacking on these matters.

Let us examine some of the Brazilian plays. Although in most developing countries of the world it is extremely difficult to secure publication for artistic works, Nascimento has been successful in having T.E.N. publication for three important books. The first, in 1961, an anthology of Negro Brazilian plays with the exquisite title, *Dramas para Negros e Prólogo para Brancos* (Plays for Blacks and a Prologue for Whites), has an excellent introduction by Nascimento, revealing the sound philosophical foundation and great learning of the man himself. The second, in 1966, a collection of reprinted theoretical articles and reviews by some of Brazil's most important critics, is called *Teatro Experimental do Negro: Testemunhos* (Testimonies). The third, *O Negro Revoltado* (The Negro in Revolt), includes the papers and declarations of the First Congress of the Brazilian Negro held in 1950, with a new introduction by Nascimento in 1968.

In the anthology of plays we find dramas written by both Blacks and Whites. Nascimento, and his Brazilian compatriots, are obviously not "hung up" on the matter of an author's race. In fact, Nascimento claims to have ready to go to press enough plays for two more anthologies of Black Brazilian drama, and at least half of the authors in them would be White. Of the nine plays in the published volume, only three are by Blacks; about the other six Nascimento writes: "perhaps they aren't by rigorous standards, really white, but, from a perspective of popular thought, they certainly are."

Surely the most important play in the volume is that by a White man, one of the leading figures in Brazilian dramaturgy. *Anjo Negro* (Black Angel), by Nelson Rodrigues, may well lay claim to being the finest specimen of Jacobean and Caroline drama in the twentieth century. Revenge, incest, bloody deeds of horror—all the necessary ingredients are there except an Italianate setting. It tells the story of a beautiful young White girl who is brought up by an aunt with five ugly daughters. She falls in love with the fiancé of her youngest cousin, and when they are caught kissing, the fiancé flees, the cousin commits suicide, and the aunt revenges herself on the very same day by sending a strapping Negro into the girl's room to "violate" her. Virginia, no longer a virgin, is forced to marry her violator, Ismael (an "outcast,"

Genesis 16:12) within the month. They subsequently have three children, all of whom Virginia murders because they are Black. Ismael, who is a doctor, has a White half brother, blind because Ismael once accidentally put the wrong medicine on his eyes. One day Elias, the brother, comes to visit, and he is seduced by Virginia because she wants a White child. Ismael kills his brother, and two years later he blinds the White child that was the product of his wife's adultery. In the last act, sixteen years later, we see that Ismael has raised this blind daughter in seclusion. Hateful of his own Blackness, he has taught her that he is the only White man left in the world and that all Negroes are to be despised. The daughter develops an unnatural love for her father, and, in a curious scene of conciliation, Virginia persuades Ismael that her daughter loves him because she believes he is White, whereas she, his wife, loves him for the Black he is. As the play closes, the daughter is placed in a glass mausoleum, and Virginia and Ismael go to bed to make another child.

When it was performed in 1948 (it had been written in 1946), *Anjo Negro* had serious problems with Brazilian censorship authorities. They insisted that the role of Ismael be played by a White actor in blackface because they were afraid that if a Negro played it he might, after the performances, go out to the streets in search of a White woman to rape. "It sounds like a funny story, but there was no humor or irony in it." The blackface was used. [26]

Another play that I believe to be important is *Aruanda*, by Joaquim Ribeiro, a White. Also written in 1946 and produced in 1948, it concerns only Black people. Rosa, a

---

culturally assimilated *mulata*, does not believe in the African cult followed by her husband, Quelé, and she is jealous of the time he spends in the ceremonies. She learns from an old *baiana* (Negress) a song in praise of the god Gangazuma, an African masculine spirit; the song begs him to come from Aruanda, the other world, to satisfy her. When Rosa sings the song in Quelé's presence, he becomes transformed into Gangazuma and adequately satisfies her sexual needs before returning to his mortal self. Eventually, Quelé comes to suspect his wife of infidelity, even though she tells him the truth, and one day in anger he punishes her by slashing her face and breasts. He knows that the gods do not like ugly women. When he is transformed again into Gangazuma, he thrusts Rosa aside and goes out looking for new women.

The play is especially interesting on several accounts. It calls for drumming musical accompaniment, and it has the character of Pai João (Old John), the Brazilian equivalent of our Uncle Remus. He has one speech that has particularly fine imagery and is worth reproducing and translating here. For those who know Portuguese, the old man's dialect will be especially interesting.

ZÉFA—Pai João, pruquê tu gosta da noite?

PAI JOÃO—Pruquê a noite é pêta, tia Zéfa. A noite é pêta, sempre foi pêta desde o meu tempo de menino, hum, hum. A noite é bonita pruquê se parece com a pele de minha gente. Hum. Hum. Branco só gosta da pretidão pra dromi pêto não. Quando eu era neguinho la na fazenda do

ZÉFA—Old John, why do you like the night?

OLD JOHN—Because the night is black, Aunt Zéfa. The night is black and always has been since I was a child, hmmm, hmmm. The night is beautiful because it looks like my people's skin. Hmmm. Whites only like blackness for sleeping, but not blacks. When I was a boy on the

209

engenho, di noite ieu fugia da senzala e ia pular no terrero, hum, hum e o feitô andava dizendo que Romã-ozinho, rondava a casa grande i era ieu. Tombém quando ieu era moleque taludo tôdas noite ieu ia bulir com as mucamas de Ya-Ya i ela se ria, inté me chamava prá bulir. Dispoz que me botaram no eito, tombém não tinha vontade de drumi. Gostava de ficar oiando as estrêlas. O intão gostava de cantar lundú. Não me ,embro! Não me lembro! Tá tão longe, tá na véia noite. A noite é pêta sim! E tão pêta que ninguem me via deitado com Maria Conguê de baixo da gameleira do outro lado do riacho, ninguém via! Noite escura esconde pêto fujão, ninguém viu quando ieu fugi pro quilombo, ninquém! Louvado seja a pretidão da noite. No fundo da noite, pêto . . . mulato . . . quiolo . . . inté brancoı Todos se parece. Me léva noite, me léva.

sugar plantation, I would escape at night from the slaves' quarters and hang around the courtyard, hmmm, hmmm, and the overseer used to say that Little Ramon was stalking the mansion, but it was really me. And when I was a little better developed I used to go every night to play around the mistress' girls, and she used to laugh. She would even send for me to come. After they put me out in the fields to work, I still had no desire to sleep. I liked to stay watching the stars. Or I would sing and dance the *lundú*. I don't remember! I don't remember! It was so long ago, there in the old night. Yes, the night is black! It's so black that nobody would see me lying down with Maria Conguê under the fig tree on the other side of the river! A black night hides the escaping black, nobody saw when I escaped to the hideout for runaway slaves, nobody! Blessed be the darkness of the night. In the deep of the night, blacks, mulattoes, coloreds, even whites—they all look alike. Night, take me with you, take me with you.

Sortilégio, a "black mystery" by Nascimento himself, has had an interesting history as a work of art. First written in 1951, several attempts to produce it met with failure because the censors refused to approve it. In 1953 the Secretariat of Public Security alleged that the play "attempted to exploit racial prejudice... [by] using language that should not be heard by any audience." The decree went

210

on to say that "the subject, treated . . . without question in a corrupt manner and in an unhealthy language, attempted to create tensions between whites and blacks, [and] was an incomprehensible racial shock, the author fleeing from the objective that he should have held to, namely, that of the search for harmony in an area so susceptible to dubious interpretations." Nascimento managed to publish the play in 1953 in *Anhembi*, the distinguished Sao Paulo literary journal, and he included with it the correspondence regarding the censorship as well as a defense of the play by Brazilian Association of Drama Critics of São Paulo. *Sortilégio* was finally produced in the Teatro Municipal, Rio, in August 1957. It is a fine play, and one truly worthy of production again if the right technical advisers can be gathered to reproduce accurately, though not naturalistically, the world of the Afro-Brazilian cult upon the stage.

The story of the play concerns a young Black lawyer, Emanuel, who is caught in the conflict between Black and White worlds. An educated man, he rejects the culture and religion of his Black heritage, and marries a White in order to secure social status. Repelled by the thought of giving birth to Emanuel's Black progeny, Margarida kills their unborn child, and she soon becomes unfaithful to her husband. In the meantime, Emanuel's Black secret love, Efigênia, a former ballet dancer who has fallen into prostitution as a result of trying to rise in her White-dominated profession by nonprofessional means, conspires against him. She persuades Emanuel to kill his faithless wife, and as the play opens he is fleeing from the police. He stumbles into a *terreiro*, a wooded clearing used for *candomblé* rituals. All the celebrants are there, and by and by the various saints and gods of the African cult appear. In a series of surrealistic events, Emanuel is forced to recall his past life, his suffering as a Negro, and his mistakes in trying to reject his heritage. Tormented by these furies, and by the specters of the two women in his life, he gives his body and soul up to the celebrants, who run him through with Exu's lance, thereby reclaiming him for the god.

A somewhat similar play is *O Castigo de Oxalá* (The Punishment of Oxalá), by Romeu Crusoé, a Negro from the northeast. This three-act play had its première in January 1961, in Rio, and is supposedly based on experiences from his own life. It tells the story of Raimundo, *"um negro forte e simpático,"* who is married to a White woman, Leonor, but is more deeply loved by a *mulata* named Rita, who quite early in the play attempts to bed him. One day, a White man who has collapsed outside the house is carried in and is invited by Raimundo to stay overnight. But his presence disturbs Leonor greatly. "You will regret it, Raimundo," she says. Sure enough, the White man turns out to be a pimp who exploited Leonor years before, is shocked to learn that she married a Negro, and now wants her back in business again. After a great deal of intrigue, Raimundo shoots at the White man, and kills Leonor whom the White man used as a shield. He then kills the intruder. The title is repeated in the words of one of the characters at the play's end. It was the punishment of the god Oxalá, a reminder to us that

Raimundo was an assimilated man who did not believe in the African cult. His tragedy is the god's revenge.

Além do Rio (Beside the River), by the White author Agostinho Olavo, is based on the Medea legend, but uses as its protagonist an African queen who was sold into slavery and brought to Brazil in the seventeenth century. Forced to become the mistress of the plantation owner, she gives him two children, but by doing so she has lost the confidence of her people. When at last her master abandons her to enter into a normal marriage with a White wife, he wishes to take the children to live with him, but the queen drowns her children in the river and returns to her people. It is an interesting play, and it is sad to report that it has yet to be produced. The Teatro Experimental do Negro attempted to take it to the First World Festival of Negro Arts at Dakar in 1966, but was not permitted to do so for reasons I shall explain shortly.

O Filho Pródigo (The Prodigal Son, 1947), by Lúcio Cardoso, another White author, was inspired by the Bible and deals with a Negro family "lost" in the vast interior of the country. Except for the father, who as a young man had walked many days and nights to the sea, no one in the family had ever seen a White person before. One night a pilgrim stops at their home for the night, and when she takes off the mysterious Black veils that cover her face, she reveals White skin with a moon-like glow. She seduces the young son, the most curious of the family, who then leaves with her for the unknown world.

I had better stop my descriptive accounts of these plays at this point and offer some general remarks regarding all of the plays in this genre.

The majority of them, clearly, deal with racially mixed love affairs or marriages. Frequently, the Black male is ashamed of, or has anxieties about, his Blackness. Likewise, the White wife or lover, though she has married out of love, has misgivings, usually related to their mutual offspring. Sexuality is a key theme running through all the plays. Most of the plays have a tragic or misfortune-ridden ending. One looks in vain for a play celebrating the joys of being Black. Its absence is revealing. Several of the plays show the mystical setting, with jungles and rushing waters, the surrealism and the probing of the subconscious that we frequently find in the negritudinous poetry of Aimé Césaire. Although none is written in formal poetic language, almost all have poetic passages interspersed throughout. These interpolations are frequently the site of the vestiges of African religion and culture. Most of the plays in the genre call for the use of folkloric songs and dances of the Negroes (*maracatu, candomblé, macumba*), and for the sounds customarily heard in Negro neighborhoods (peddlers, street urchins).

But T.E.N. is more than just a producer of plays—it is an idea, and one of the few active examples of *negritude* in Brazil. The goals of T.E.N. are obvious: (1) to "cultivate Africanness within the Brazilian theater, (2) to attract more Negro audience members to the theater, and (3) to foster the development of studies of the Negro in society. To forward these ends, T.E.N. sponsored *Quilombo*, a journal devoted to Negro culture which appeared from late 1948 through 1950.

It encouraged and sometimes provided the actors for productions of plays about Blacks in the regular theaters of Rio and São Paulo. It gave literacy and culture courses to over 600 persons. It organized the National Negro Conventions in São Paulo in 1945 and in Rio in 1946, as well as the First Congress of the Brazilian Negro, held in 1950, the proceedings of which have recently appeared in print. In 1955 it sponsored a "Negro Week," which included a contest for artists dealing with the theme of the Black Christ, and in 1967 it founded a Museum of Negro Art which carries on even today. For a number of years it sponsored Black beauty contests, choosing a "Rainha das Mulatas" (Queen of the Mulattoes) and a "Boneca de Pixe" (Tar Doll), because it felt that a "social tactic and a pedagogic instrument" was needed to integrate Black women into national contests of this type.[27]

It is clear, then, that T.E.N. has been more than just a theater—it has been the cultural headquarters of negritude in Brazil. And its leader, Abdias do Nascimento, has been the unflagging racial conscience of his country. Brazilian intellectuals realize that Nascimento is one of the few, if not the only one, who fights in every way against prejudice, against paternalism, and in favor of the advancement of the Negro in all sectors of Brazilian life.[28] The fact that his ideas are generally met with hostility and suspicion does not discourage Nascimento; he responds: "The Experimental Theatre of the Negro is a process. Negritude is a process."[29]

But what are the realities? Can negritude really take root in Brazil? Roger Bastide, the eminent French sociologist who knows Brazil intimately, argues that because of the absence of legal barriers regulating race relations, and because of the mixed racial ancestry of many Brazilians, any movement, whether negritude, or "literary Africanitude," as Bastide calls it, is bound to fail. The antagonistic cultural polarities it creates are simply not acceptable to large numbers of people.[30] This view finds corroboration in the fact that in Portuguese Africa, which has a different racial reality, Black poets are deeply concerned with revolt and indignation, and are committed to political separation. In the case of an anthology of Afro-Portuguese poetry published in the early 1960s, fifteen out of the eighteen poets represented were in prison or in exile.[31] While it is true that many of Brazil's intellectual class are presently in exile because of stern measures imposed by a strong, military-led government, I have not discovered any charges to the effect that racial considerations were at play here. The fact that a recent law prohibits the dissemination of information which might provoke racial disharmony does not mean that a racial revolt is underway in Brazil. Such an action must instead be seen as just another manifestation of oversensitivity on the part of leaders who are perfectionists and who perhaps unrealistically seek perfect tranquility in all sectors of that vast country.

As Abdias do Nascimento's thinking and philosophical development have evolved over the last two and a half decades, they are in direct opposition to current government policy. Perhaps that is why he prefers to remain out of Brazil for the present. In 1968-1969 he was a visiting lecturer at Yale University's School of Drama, and in 1969-1970 he was a Visiting Fellow at the Center for the Humanities at Wesleyan University. The conflict between T.E.N. and the government is purely a philosophical one, for Nascimento and T.E.N. have assiduously avoided political entanglements. There is no doubt that Brazilian society is gradually "blending" from a racial point of view. The number of pure Blacks is declining for various reasons. Some call this a "bleaching" process, and look upon it favorably since they think that it means an essentially White society for Brazil in the future.[32] The government shares this view, and in fact it has eliminated all questions on race for the 1970 census. On the other side are those who hold that "racial assimilation is mulattoization rather than Aryanization."[33] They claim to wish "not to polarize the races but simply to vindicate the common dignity of all races in a *mestiço* society." They reject total cultural assimilation just as today in the United States many people are concerned about the disappearance of the hyphenated American. Some Brazilian Blacks have joined a sociopolitical movement which holds this philosophy, and has as its structure such organizations as the "Brazilian Negro Union," "The Brazilian Movement Against Racial Prejudice," and the "Union of Colored People." But these are not yet the powerful lobbying organizations that we find among parallel groups in the United States. And they will not be if, as Brazil takes its place among the Western industrial and commercial powers and imports the technological idealogies of the more developed nations, it is able to prevent the simultaneous importation of unfavorable Western attitudes and concepts of race.

With a government policy of long standing against racially based organizations, especially those groups who want to remind the power structure that an unusually high percentage of the nation's poor are Black; with a population that has an illiteracy level that some suggest is between 50 and 70 percent of the whole; with a national language, Portuguese, that acts as a linguistic obstacle against reading world literature at home (for not everything is translated into Portuguese), and that prevents the good artistic works of Brazil from being easily exported; with a Black population that in the main is not aware of its situation, and that shows no sign of incipient militancy—can we honestly be sanguine about the future?

In 1966, when Itamarati (the Brazilian Ministry of Foreign Affairs) chose the groups and individuals to represent Brazil at the First World Festival of Negro Arts at Dakar, Senegal, it refused to allow the Teatro Experimental do Negro to go. The selection committee issued a document stating its philosophy, the first requirement of which was "a criterion of national integration." It unilaterally disqualified any Afro-Brazilian art which represented "a return to the origins," since, it said, this is an artificialism that does not represent "the living and present values of our heritage." Of course, the "return to the origins" was one of the objectives of the entire Dakar Festival. The document went on to justify sending only those groups that had "a prospective outlook," one recognizing "the extreme mobility" and the "very wide process of acculturation in Brazil." The document concluded: "No problem of revival is posed for Brazil, but only the permanence of Negro values under the common denominator of acculturation." It would have been simpler to say straightaway that the government wanted to keep from Dakar those who would paint too black a picture of the "integrated" artistic world in Brazil. Nascimento wrote an Open Letter protesting the committee's decision, and sent copies to the Festival participants, UNESCO, and the president of Senegal. The letter even found its way into the pages of *Présence Africaine*. But it did little good. I think Nascimento's heart may have broken a little bit as a result of these events. Although his museum has opened since then, T.E.N. has not produced a play or sponsored a conference or run a beauty contest or issued a journal since 1966. Whether it will again or not, only the Orixás know.

NOTES

1. Abdias do Nascimento, *The Orixás. Afro-Brazilian Paintings and Text* (Middletown, Conn.: Malcolm X House of the Afro-American Institute, Wesleyan University, 1969), p. 3.

2. *Encyclopaedia Britannica Book of the Year, 1970* (Chicago, 1970), p. 177.

3. Charles Wagley, ed., *Race and Class in Rural Brazil* (Paris, 1952), p. 142. Also see E. Franklin Frazier, "A Comparison of Negro-White Relations in Brazil and in the United States," *Transactions of the New York Academy of Sciences* (1944): 251-269. For more recent reports, see Marvin Harris, "Racial Identity in Brazil," *Luso-Brazilian Review* (1964): 21-28, and Magnus Mörner, "The History of Race Relations in Latin America: Some Comments on the State of Research," *Latin American Research Review* (1966): 17-44.

4. Charles Wagley, *Race and Class*, p. 154.

5. Ibid., p. 130.

6. Octavio Ianni, "Raça e classe," Educaçao e Ciencias Sociais (Rio), no. 19 (January-April 1962): 88-111; quoted in United Nations Economic Commission for Latin America, *Education, Human Resources and Development in Latin America* (New York, 1968), p. 83.

7. Charles Wagley, *Race and Class*, p. 121.

8. Ben Zimmerman, "Race Relations in the Arid Sertao." In Charles Wagley, *Race and Class*, pp. 94-95, 97; Charles Wagley, *Race and Class*, p. 121; Abdias do Nascimento, ed., *O Negro Revoltado* (Rio de Janeiro, 1968), p. 138; Pierre Joffroy, *Brazil*, trans. Douglas Garman (New York, Viking, 1965), p. 138.

9. Charles Wagley, *Race and Class*, p. 121.

10. Ben Zimmerman, "Race Relations," p. 95.

11. Guerreiro Ramos, "Patologia Social do 'Branco' Brasileiro," quoted in Abdias do Nascimento, "The Negro Theatre in Brazil," *African Forum* 2(1967): 44.

12. Charles Wagley, *Race and Class* p. 153.

13. Ben Zimmerman, "Race Relations," p. 94.

14 Mário de Andrade, *Danças Dramáticas do Brasil*, 3 vols. (Sao Paulo, 1959).

15. Abdias do Nascimento, "The Negro Theatre in Brazil," p. 39; Abdias do Nascimento, ed., *Dramas para Negros e Prólogo para Brancos; antologia do teatro negro-brasileiro* (Rio de Janeiro, 1961), p. 21.

16. Michael J. C. Echeruo, "Concert and Theatre in Late Nineteenth Century Lagos," *Nigeria Magazine*, no. 74 (September 1962): 68.

17. Ibid., pp. 69-70.

18. Janheinz Jahn, *A History of Neo-African Literature. Writing in Two Continents*, trans. Oliver Coburn and Ursula Lehrburger (London, Faber 1968), p. 15.

19. Ibid., p. 125.

20. Ibid., p. 121.

21. Abdias do Nascimento, "Negro Theater in Brazil," *Américas* 1(June 1949): 23; Abdias do Nascimento, *The Orixás, p. 2.*

22. Abdias do Nascimento, "The Negro Theatre in Brazil," *African Forum* 2(1967), p. 35.

23. Ibid., p. 36.

24. Abdias do Nascimento, "Negro Theater in Brazil," *Americas* 1(June 1949), p. 22.

25. Ibid., p. 23.

26. Abdias do Nascimento, "The Negro Theatre in Brazil," p. 47.

27. Abdias do Nascimento, *The Orixás*, p. 3.

28. Antônio Olinto, "The Negro Writer and the Negro Influence in Brazilian Literature," *African Forum* 2(1967): 17.

29. Abdias do Nascimento, "The Negro Theatre in Brazil," p. 53.

30. Richard A. Prêto-Rodas, *"The Development of Negritude in the* Poetry of the Portuguese Speaking World." In *Artists and Writers in the Evolution of Latin America*, edited by Edward Davis Terry (University of Alabama Press, 1969), p. 58, quoting Bastide, "Variations sur la Négritude," *Présence Africaine*, 36 (1961): 8.

31. Ibid., p. 61.

32. Charles Wagley, *Race and Class*, p. 153; Pierre Joffroy, *Brazil*, p. 144.

33. Richard Prêto-Rodas, "The Development of Negritude," p. 59; Abdias do Nascimento, *Dramas para Negros*, p. 21.

221

NOTES ON CONTRIBUTORS

John F. Bayliss is originally from Great Britain, and is now Associate Professor of English at Indiana State University. In addition to several papers on Black literature and English, he has edited the anthology, *Black Slave Narratives*. He is also editor of the journal, *Negro American Literature Forum*.

Lloyd W. Brown, a Jamaican, is Associate Professor of English and Comparative Literature at the University of Southern California. He taught in Canada before immigrating to the United States, and has written several articles on Black literature and English. He is now working on a book-length study of the Black revolution in American literature, and is coediting an anthology of essays on Pan-African writing.

Abraham Chapman, Professor of English at Wisconsin State University, is the editor of the anthology, *Black Voices*, and its forthcoming sequel, *New Black Voices*. He is also working on a collection of Afro-American slave narratives for future publication.

Austin C. Clarke is originally from Barbados, but now lives permanently in Toronto, Canada. He is the author of three novels, *Survivors of the Crossing, Among Thistles and Thorns*, and *Meeting Point*, as well as a forthcoming collection of short stories. He has been a visiting Professor of English at Yale University and at Williams College, Massachusetts.

Mercer A. Cook is Professor of Romance Languages at Howard University and a visiting Professor in the Department of Romance Languages, Harvard University. In addition to a distinguished academic career, Professor Cook has served as the United States Ambassador to Niger (1961) and to Senegal (1964). His numerous publications include *Le Noir, Five French Negro Authors, Education in Haiti, The Militant Black Writer in Africa and the United States* (with Stephen Henderson). He has also translated Mamadou Dia's *African Nations and World Solidarity* and Leopold Senghor's *On African Socialism*.

James A. Emanuel is Associate Professor of English at City College, New York. He is the coeditor of *Dark Symphony: Negro Literature in America,* and has authored the full-length study, *Langston Hughes,* in the Twayne's United States Authors Series. A collection of his poetry has been published as *The Treehouse and Other Poems.*

Nick Aaron Ford is Chairman of the Department of English at Morgan State College. He has written numerous papers on Black American literature, as well as a pioneering study, *The Contemporary Negro Novel* (1936). He is the editor of *Black Insights: Significant Literature by Afro-Americans.*

Ismith Khan is a Trinidadian novelist whose works include *Jumbie Bird* and *Obeah Man.* He has taught at the New School, New York, and at Johns Hopkins University. He is now in the Third College, University of California at San Diego. Mr. Khan is also the author of several short stories published in American journals.

Frederic M. Litto is Associate Professor of English at the University of Kansas where he is also the director of the International Theatre Studies Center. He founded and formerly edited the *Afro-Asian Theatre Bulletin.* Moreover, he is the coeditor of *Latin American Theatre Review,* which he also founded, and editor of *Theatre Documentation.* His publications include a bibliography, *American Dissertations on the Drama and the Theatre,* and an anthology, *Plays from Black Africa.*

Edward Margolies is Associate Professor of English at Staten Island Community College. A Richard Wright specialist, he is the author of *The Art of Richard Wright* and is working on an edition of *The Letters of Richard Wright*. He has also written a collection of essays on Black American literature, *Native Sons,* and is now working on a study of the Harlem Renaissance.

INDEX

Achebe, Chinua, 36, 38.
Achille, Louis T., 121, 124.
Anthony, Michael, 174-176, 181-182, 183.
Armstrong, Louis, "Satchmo", 125-126.
Attaway, William, 95.
Baldwin, James, 6-7, 26-27, 67, 135.
Beti, Mongo, 133.
Black Aesthetic, 3-5, 7-8, 11-40, 98.
Black American Music, 12, 14, 23-24, 121, 124-126.

Black Christ, 128-129.
Black Media, 13-15.
Black Muslims, 188.
Black Nationalism, 8, 112, 177-178, 188.
Black Power, 76-78, 112, 192.
Black Revolution, 6, 53.
Black Studies, 70-72, 75-79, 82-83.
Bone, Robert A., 6, 61-63, 81-82, 86.
Bontemps, Arna, 63, 86, 95.
Brathwaite, Edward, 187-188, 190, 193.

227

228